THE BASICS

Literary Analysis: The Basics is an insightful introduction to analysing a wide range of literary forms. Providing a clear outline of the methodologies employed in twenty-first-century literary analysis, it introduces readers to the genres, canons, terms, issues, critical approaches, and contexts that affect the analysis of any text. It addresses such questions as:

- What counts as literature?
- Is analysis a dissection?
- How do gender, race, class, and culture affect the meaning of a text?
- Why is the social and historical context of a text important?
- Can digital media be analysed in the same way as a poem?

With examples ranging from ancient myths to young adult fiction, a glossary of key terms, and suggestions for further reading, *Literary Analysis: The Basics* is essential reading for anyone wishing to improve their analytical reading skills.

Celena Kusch is Associate Professor of American Literature at the University of South Carolina Upstate, USA.

THE BASICS

ACTING
BELLA MERLIN

AMERICAN PHILOSOPHY
NANCY STANLICK

ANCIENT NEAR EAST
DANIEL C. SNELL

ANIMAL ETHICS
TONY MILLIGAN

ANTHROPOLOGY
PETER METCALF

ARCHAEOLOGY (SECOND EDITION)
CLIVE GAMBLE

ART HISTORY
GRANT POOKE AND DIANA NEWALL

ARTIFICIAL INTELLIGENCE
KEVIN WARWICK

THE BIBLE
JOHN BARTON

THE BIBLE AND LITERATURE
NORMAN W. JONES

BIOETHICS
ALASTAIR V. CAMPBELL

BODY STUDIES
NIALL RICHARDSON AND ADAM LOCKS

BRITISH POLITICS
BILL JONES

BUDDHISM
CATHY CANTWELL

CAPITALISM
DAVID COATES

CHRISTIANITY
BRUCE CHILTON

THE CITY
KEVIN ARCHER

CONTEMPORARY LITERATURE
SUMAN GUPTA

CRIMINAL LAW
JONATHAN HERRING

CRIMINOLOGY (SECOND EDITION)
SANDRA WALKLATE

DANCE STUDIES
JO BUTTERWORTH

EASTERN PHILOSOPHY
VICTORIA S. HARRISON

ECONOMICS (THIRD EDITION)
TONY CLEAVER

EDUCATION
KAY WOOD

ENERGY
MICHAEL SCHOBERT

EUROPEAN UNION (SECOND EDITION)
ALEX WARLEIGH-LACK

EVOLUTION
SHERRIE LYONS

FILM STUDIES (SECOND EDITION)
AMY VILLAREJO

FINANCE (THIRD EDITION)
ERIK BANKS

FOOD ETHICS
RONALD SANDLER

FREE WILL
MEGHAN GRIFFITH

GENDER
HILARY LIPS

LITERARY ANALYSIS
THE BASICS

Celena Kusch

Routledge
Taylor & Francis Group

LONDON AND NEW YORK

First published 2016
by Routledge
2 Park Square, Milton Park, Abingdon, Oxon OX14 4RN

and by Routledge
711 Third Avenue, New York, NY 10017

Routledge is an imprint of the Taylor & Francis Group, an informa business

© 2016 Celena Kusch

British Library Cataloguing-in-Publication Data
A catalogue record for this book is available from the British Library

Library of Congress Cataloging-in-Publication Data
Names: Kusch, Celena.Title: Literary analysis: the basics/Celena Kusch.
Description: Milton Park, Abingdon, Oxon; New York: Routledge, 2016. | Includes bibliographical references and index.
Identifiers: LCCN 2015034080| ISBN 9780415747097 (hardback: alk. paper) | ISBN 9780415747103 (pbk. : alk. paper) | ISBN 9781315688374 (ebook)
Subjects: LCSH: Literature—Philosophy. | Literary form. | Literature—History and criticism—Theory, etc.
Classification: LCC PN45 .K834 2016 | DDC 801—dc23LC record available at http://lccn.loc.gov/2015034080

ISBN: 978-0-415-74709-7 (hbk)
ISBN: 978-0-415-74710-3 (pbk)
ISBN: 978-1-315-68837-4 (ebk)

Typeset in Bembo
by Book Now Ltd, London

CONTENTS

INTRODUCTION: THINKING ABOUT LITERATURE

WHAT IS LITERATURE?

From ancient myths and oral stories to today's fan fiction and self-publishing boom, literature has served a variety of functions in society. Literature conveys sacred knowledge, teaches moral and social lessons, announces new ideas, records revolutions, tests the limits of cultural values, and shows us our best and worst selves. As the set of stories we tell of ourselves through **narrative**, **performance**, **lyrical** reflection, and many other forms, literature encapsulates human experience and records the messy, painful, triumphant, and sublime realities of the passage of humans through our world. While other fields of study attempt to understand humans by measuring and compiling facts about our psychological responses, economic behaviours, sociological institutions, and anthropological patterns, those fields smooth out the edges of our rough and often irrational behaviours by highlighting general tendencies or statistical probabilities. Literature offers us the human life in total – not reduced – with its inconsistent logic, morality, and identity on full display.

For instance, when William Shakespeare's *Macbeth* was first performed in 1606, three years after Queen Elizabeth I's death, the play provided an imaginative forum from which to consider and debate questions of power, gender, ambition, political machination, and the nation itself.

Three centuries later, when the play was staged in 1936 Harlem with an African American cast, *Macbeth* became an emblem of African American artistic equality and a revolutionary statement about shifts in racial, artistic, and political power in the USA. A 1970 Zulu-language adaptation of the play had an even more radical effect for South Africans. Playwright Welcome Msomi rewrote *Macbeth* as *uMabatha*, the story of Shaka Zulu, a nineteenth-century Zulu ruler. This translation and revision of Shakespeare's text brought new attention to the achievements, intrigue, ambition, and ultimate tragedy of this period of South Africa's history.

The gender issues at the heart of the original play have also resurfaced again and again. In particular, the 1955 Vivien Leigh and Laurence Olivier stage performance at Stratford-upon-Avon – Shakespeare's home – spotlighted the role of Lady Macbeth. Olivier's planned film adaptation would have further redefined Lady Macbeth's femininity and ambition by adding a miscarriage to the plot (Barnes 2012).

Finally, imperialism, modernization, and culture came to the fore in the presentations of *Macbeth* embedded in the 1965 Merchant Ivory film, *Shakespeare Wallah*. The film, set in India, depicts the lives of the actors in a travelling Shakespeare company whose work is being replaced by a home-grown Bollywood film industry. The film questions the role of the English literary tradition in an independent India, but, like the play it quotes, offers no easy answers.

So what keeps readers, writers, and audiences coming back to this play in so many different forms and so many different times? Is it that we, like Macbeth, want to know the point of power and ambition in our brief lives? Do we want to know if it is true that 'Life's but a walking shadow, a poor player/That struts and frets his hour upon the stage/And then is heard no more' (Shakespeare 2008, act 5, scene 5, lines 24–6)? Or are we more interested in identifying the 'Something wicked' that 'this way comes' (Shakespeare 2008, act 4, scene 1, line 45)?

Both the original play, *Macbeth*, and later adaptations call upon readers and audiences to examine the meaning of human experience by using rich language to inspire thoughts and feelings in each of us. Indeed, literary **critic**s for centuries have highlighted the personal effects of reading literature. Nineteenth-century critic Matthew Arnold viewed the study of literature as a path to attaining humanity's best quality, culture, which he described in

Culture and Anarchy (1869) as our spiritual quest for 'sweetness and light' through beauty, knowledge, and the rational pursuit of truth. More recently, Harold Bloom (2001, p. 22) called reading 'selfish rather than social', as readers enjoy the beautiful words that inspire their interests and their sense of self. Critic Rita Felski (2008) claims that we use literature to recognize ourselves in the words of others, to gain knowledge, to experience shock, and to feel a sense of enchantment with new worlds and new ways of seeing our own – all uses attuned to the reactions brewing in the individual reader's mind.

Without a doubt, much of the magic of literature lies in this capacity to transform a single life. But not all.

As a social medium and a technology for sharing words, images, and ideas, literature ignites another kind of magic. Literature offers us an immersive record of our past and emerging collective experience. Shared readings establish points of contact that cross national, historical, linguistic, and cultural boundaries.

Before written language, the earliest oral literature – creation stories and epics of early tribes and civilizations – was recited and performed in memorable language with rhythmic beats to preserve and circulate the core knowledge and identities of groups of people. To borrow Felski's terms, the wave of enchantment of these early spoken texts carried essential knowledge, recognition, belonging, and even shock at actions that could threaten the survival of the community as a whole. Today, with over seven billion people living in approximately 200 nations around the globe, such strictly unifying messages are neither possible nor desirable, yet the connections forged through literature continue to serve vital, collective functions in our diverse and complex societies.

The examples above define what literature *does*, not what it *is*. The paragraphs that follow map out a few approaches to facing a definition of literature head-on.

Earlier I stated that literature is a social medium and a technology for sharing words, images, and ideas. This definition is very broad, and under it, we might call Web sites or mobile apps like Facebook or Instagram examples of literature. Clearly, we need to refine.

Literature is a set of **text**s (a general term for objects made of words, no matter what their format) whose purpose includes, but extends beyond, communication, in which the language itself is as much a part of the end product as is the content. Those texts might include everything from lyric poetry to feature films and television series that use language not only in the typed screenplays but also in the spoken performances of script and body language and in the relationship between the words and screen images. Box 1.1 includes a small sampling of literary technologies from our past and present.

BOX 1.1 LITERARY TECHNOLOGIES OF THE PAST AND PRESENT

oral storytelling	comedy	tragedy
drama	letters	illuminated
sermons	histories	manuscripts
biographies	epic poetry	travel writing
lyric poetry	oratory	*haiku*
Vedas	series in magazines	satires
short stories	slave narratives	sketches
novels	fan fiction	memoirs
pulp fiction	radio plays	graphic novels
film	rap	television series
opera	flash fiction	hypertext poetry
diy film	sacred hymns/	slam poetry
song lyrics	prayers	

Again, it is easy to make the definition of literature overwhelmingly broad; to paraphrase Raymond Williams (1976), the trouble comes when we attempt to exclude individual texts or types of texts from the category of literature.

Initially, such exclusions were not part of the definition at all. In communities with a low level of **literacy** and limited supplies of expensive writing materials, literature meant merely 'that which was written', including everything from philosophical reflections and histories to poetry or plays. By the 1700s in Europe, that definition began to narrow to only 'well-written' or '**literary**' texts of various sorts, adding elements of style, taste, class status, and social value to the definition – values that continue to foster debate today.

For Western literature, the Romanticists of the early nineteenth century added an emphasis on creativity and imagination, further narrowing the field at precisely the time that literacy rates and inexpensive print media were gaining ground. As Terry Eagleton (2008, p. 17) explains in 'The Rise of English', poets like Samuel Taylor Coleridge and Percy Bysshe Shelley sought to make literature 'a mysterious organic unity' that could transcend the practical and material realities of daily life through inspiration and genius. This distinction can be described as the difference between literature with a lowercase *l* – the stuff of celebrity biographies, romance novels, and detective fiction available for purchase alongside tabloids in a grocery store – and Literature with an uppercase *L*, the elite product of artists of language, the work of literary geniuses who appeal to advanced readers with 'higher' concerns.

Today, literature remains a contested term. We can agree with Eagleton (2008, p. 9) that literature is 'a highly valued kind of writing', but we rarely agree on which values to apply. Those who espouse definitions of *Literature*, often exclude the more populist and democratic media used to produce certain texts – such as television, film, popular fiction, graphic novels, popular music lyrics, video game narratives, and the like. Those who advocate definitions of *literature* often embrace newer literary forms, but trip over examples at the fringes or extremes.

Does the 2014 film sequel *Sharknado 2: The Second One* – a disaster movie about dangerous, salt-water cyclones filled with live and hungry sharks – fit the definition of literature? In some ways, I truly hope not. Yet, the vitality of literature as a field stems from our willingness to adapt and respond to the changing institutions for producing, publishing, distributing, accessing, and connecting through language. As an object of analysis, *Sharknado 2* or films like it could play a valuable role in our ongoing attempt to refine our understanding of what literature is and what purpose it serves for our world in our time and in generations to come.

Ultimately, excluding or including particular texts from the definition of literature is not my aim in this book. I ask only that we recognize that approaching any text as literature means attending to it as a product made of language that responds to and represents some slice of our world in ways that are not readily apparent in a single, surface-level reading. Regardless of the definition we individually adopt – whether it be *literature* or *Literature* – the tools of literary analysis outlined in this book are applicable to whatever texts we read.

ANALYSIS, CLASSICS, AND THE LITERARY CANON

The experience of literature is both emotional and intellectual, both felt and known. In private, literature can and perhaps should be purely subjective. We feel the joy and anguish of the characters whose stories we read. The descriptions of faraway places or lyrical reflections on the human condition all engage our senses and open our hearts and minds to new possibilities that both connect to and transcend our daily lives. Our favourite books are as entwined in our personal memories and identities as our favourite songs.

But in public discussions and formal literary study, we require ways to bridge individual, emotional responses and to go beyond subjectivity to uncover new insights about the meanings of various texts. We need collective rules and assumptions and a shared vocabulary to describe literary effects. In short, we need tools to break large texts into their component parts in order to analyse the way literature is written, why it is written that way, and what it means – far beyond simply a history of the words or an outline of the author's conscious attempts to craft the text. We need a systematic practice like literary analysis to allow us to understand how literature is written, why it is written that way, and what effects these details have on meaning as a whole.

It may be somewhat surprising, then, to consider that the academic tradition of literary analysis in English is not even 200 years old.

In the Judeo-Christian tradition, the first scholars to use the methods that would become the foundation of literary analysis were theologians, and their texts were the Hebrew and Greek scriptures of the Tanakh or Bible. Practising *hermeneutics*, the theory of finding meaning through interpretation, these clerics produced *exegesis*, the critical explanation of the meaning of a text. St. Augustine's multi-volume *Tractates on the Gospel of John* (*c.* 406–420), for example, offers a line-by-line exegesis of the entire gospel, beginning with several pages exploring how the Word both was 'with God' and 'was God' (John 1:1). Theologians like St. Augustine based their explanations of sacred literature on careful analysis of the following:

- historical information about the author and the events in the period being depicted;
- the origins, translations, and idiomatic or figurative meanings of the particular words in the passage;
- comparisons with other passages about the same content or within the same part of the text;
- and comparisons among different ancient manuscripts of the same text.

Many of these methodologies still inform the practice of literary analysis today.

For centuries, though, the only texts considered worthy of analysis were sacred writings. Even among these writings, only the **canonical** literature (also called the **canon**), the set of sacred books and theological documents deemed authentic and officially approved by the religious leadership, were viewed as acceptable subjects of exegesis and analysis. It is from this model of the religious canon that the academic institution of the literary canon evolved.

When we discuss the **literary canon**, we refer to a set of literary texts widely recognized for their importance, influence, brilliance, and exemplary qualities – criteria that are notoriously subjective and value-laden. Unlike the biblical canon, however, there is no definitive list and no single authority to generate and regulate such a list. We find these lists informally in the major anthologies of literature, in the syllabi of university courses, in the required readings for qualifying examinations and certification tests, in the curriculum guides for secondary schools, in publications of literary **criticism**, and in the general icons of literary history represented in monuments, museums, films, and public culture. As the record of both public and expert interest, the literary canon expands and contracts as the definition of literature and our collective sense of its value shifts over time.

To illustrate: in England, after scholars began to embrace secular literature as part of academic study, they turned their attention to classical literature in Latin and Greek, performing literary exegesis of Homer's *Iliad* and *Odyssey* (8th century BCE) or Virgil's *Aeneid* (c. 19 BCE) in much the same way (and in many of the same languages) that biblical exegesis had been performed. Throughout most of the Renaissance, academic authorities saw no need to analyze texts written in English, whose meaning was viewed as accessible without rigorous study.

By the eighteenth century, the authors themselves were well on their way to creating a canon of English literature. Samuel Johnson's *Lives of the Poets* (1779–1781) is the most famous example of such an effort to establish at least a partial canon for readers, if not for universities. In fact, Gerald Graff (2007) points out that by the early nineteenth century, communities of literary clubs, debating societies, and magazine readers and contributors actively engaged the field of English literature as part of their everyday social activities throughout many English-speaking nations. Famous public lectures – such as the 1806 and 1810 lectures by Coleridge on Shakespeare's *Hamlet* – sketched the shape of the canon before large audiences. In turn, Graff notes, academic scholars generally felt the field of English literature (much like popular television today) belonged to the public, not to university experts.

Within educational institutions, the study of classical Greek and Latin literature focused increasingly on grammar and the field of *philology*, the study of the historical development of language and its evolving structures and meanings as expressed in literature. These practices later became the nineteenth-century model for English studies which focused mostly on Old and Middle English and the development of the language or on historical criticism about the authors' lives and accomplishments. Based on these academic interests, the canon inside the university tilted more in favour of older texts – *Beowulf, The Pearl, Sir Gawain and the Green Knight* – than on the works of the writers of the time.

Both inside and outside the university, the field of English and world literatures has shifted considerably. If we fast forward to the late twentieth century, we find the literary canon a site of intense scholarly dispute. Certainly, some of the same writers who drew the attention of earlier critics and scholars remained in the canon of the 1980s and 1990s: Geoffrey Chaucer, William Shakespeare, Edmund Spenser, and John Milton, to name just a few. The works of these authors have often been described as English **classic**s, texts that can be read as 'masterpieces' of literary craft; texts that address ideas of fundamental importance with such eloquence that they transcend place and time; in short, 'Great Literature'. Such terms, like the notion of the canon itself, rely on value judgments designed to erect borders around the best and separate it from the rest. In reaction, the trend of the twenty-first century has been to 'open' the canon, break down borders, and question the power structures that promote some authors or some groups of authors over others.

Among Johnson's 52 English poets in his *Lives*, for example, only five are Welsh, Scottish, or Anglo-Irish. None is a woman. None comes from British colonies. Nearly all attended one of a handful of exclusive schools. Lists like Johnson's have led many to call the English literary canon the tradition of great white men. When Virginia Woolf (1981) levelled her criticism of the canon in *A Room of One's Own* in 1929, she pointed to several factors that had limited the role of women in literature:

- women were excluded from public places, such as schools, libraries, and theatres, in which they could be exposed to literary communities;
- cultural expectations of femininity established silence and modesty as women's greatest achievements;
- property laws prevented women from gaining financial independence and affording themselves the luxury of time and space in which to write uninterrupted; and
- male-dominated institutions did not recognize the value of women's perspectives and voices and therefore did not publish, compensate, promote, or reward women's literature.

Woolf offers as an example, the fictionalized figure of Shakespeare's sister, born with as much raw talent and intellect as her famous brother, but destined to meet a tragic and silent end because she could not go to school, could not write except in secret, and could not gain access to the theatre except as the mistress of a stage manager. What I find most interesting about Woolf's argument and example is that they are systemic, not personal. For Woolf, no single authority chose male writers over female, wealthy over poor, privileged over marginalized. Yet the set of social and political institutions that make the fields of literature and literary study possible reproduced power inequalities (based on gender, race, nationality, religion, class, sexuality, etc.) within the literary canon as well.

Echoing Woolf's institutional criticisms, scholars of the late twentieth century ultimately concluded that the canon is not an objective classification system, but that our views of 'greatness', 'importance', and 'universalism' have always been influenced by society's power structures.

Individual texts make their way into the canon because they offer representative examples of the dominant **movement**s, **genre**s, experiments and innovations, and/or intellectual trends at the time, but that 'dominance' depends upon society's values. As a result, today scholars and critics engage in spirited debates about the best way to reshape the literary canon to reflect those texts of greatest literary value – the books that everyone must read – without falling into the traps of discrimination or marginalization that have so sharply limited our literary history. Books like John Guillory's *Cultural Capital: The Problem of Literary Canon Formation* (1993), Leslie Fiedler and Houston Baker's *English Literature: Opening up the Canon* (1981), and Sandra Gilbert and Susan Gubar's *The Madwoman in the Attic* (1979) and *No Man's Land: The Place of the Women Writer in the Twentieth Century* (1988, 1994) all offer possible corrections and additions to the short list of classics that make up the canon. They call into question the criteria used to divide between 'dominant' and 'minor' literary texts and bring additional **movement**s and **genre**s, to the fore.

The result of these debates is that major anthologies of English or American literature now include female, multicultural, and transnational writers in nearly all **literary period**s: we read Margery Kempe beside Chaucer, Olaudah Equiano on the heels of Aphra Behn, and a parade of postcolonial and multicultural Nobel Laureates – Derek Walcott, Toni Morrison, J. M. Coetzee, Rabindranath Tagore, V. S. Naipaul, Nadine Gordimer – in studies of twentieth-century literature in English. Likewise, the world literature anthologies have grown increasingly global, spanning East, West, North, and South in the authors, movements, and selected texts.

After this history of controversy, expansion, and change, we might ask why bother with a literary canon at all? And what effect does the canon have upon the process of literary analysis?

The answer is threefold. Practically speaking, without it, students could not reasonably study for exams and instructors would teach endless courses; scholars could not count on a shared familiarity with any of the texts in their articles and books; and editors and publishers would be forced into capricious or arbitrary decisions about anthology contents, press catalogues, and even the list of texts kept in print. The canon places manageable limits upon the enormous amount of content that could be included in a study of literature and creates a common foundation from which to build expertise within the literary field. The canon makes our academic institutions run more smoothly.

The canon also keeps in circulation texts that have historically influenced and shaped the work of writers in later literary movements and times. It reminds us that the literature we read and love was produced by writers who also read and loved earlier literature. Can we read Walcott's *Omeros* without knowing Homer? Certainly. But the poem is much more interesting if we have *The Iliad* and *Odyssey* on our bookshelves too. Can we read Rita Dove's *Mother Love* without Ovid, Petrarch, and Shakespeare? Of course. But the earth will move beneath our feet far more if we recognize the whispers of the canon within Dove's poems.

Finally, knowing what is or is not in the canon makes us more aware of the potential political implications of our own analyses. As Frank Kermode (1989, p. 115) states in 'Canon and Period', 'canons are complicit with power', and they function by 'affirming that some works are more valuable than others, more worthy of minute attention'. When we direct our attention to more marginal texts, no matter what else we might be saying, we are also making an argument that our collective sense of literary value should change. Predominantly defined by academic interests, the contemporary canon is often at odds with public reading practices and literary discussions beyond the university walls. Knowledge of the canon provides readers with a touchstone of accepted interpretations and evaluations of different categories of literature; it offers an entry point into critical conversations about the literature that matters to us – whether it be canonical or not.

Put another way, we cannot change the canon unless we know the canon and the various institutional functions it serves and that support it. Even many texts which today hold a central place as 'classics' within the canon had been disregarded or viewed as too popular or marginal by previous generations. Changes brought about by later writers, critics, publishers, and scholars can all contribute to a shift in institutional status and either bury significant literature of the past or make previously noncanonical texts emerge as exemplary of their literary categories.

Poet, novelist, and playwright John Masefield, for instance, served as the UK's Poet Laureate from 1930–1967. He was a member of W. B. Yeats's circle of writers and friends, but his pre-First World War aesthetic has not given him enduring influence in the literary canon. Masefield wrote sonnets and ballads, social novels, novels of sea travel, religious plays and children's literature – both content and forms that fit better with our concepts of the nineteenth century than the early twentieth. Today he is best known for his children's books, and the Modern Language Association's bibliography of scholarly articles and books lists only five new texts about Masefield in this century. Certainly, Masefield impressed the powerful literary institutions of an earlier time, but he is not a canonical British author today due to changes in society's values and interests.

In contrast, the writing of modernist poet and novelist H.D. (Hilda Doolittle) played a significant role in early twentieth-century literary experimentation. She contributed to important magazines as both editor and critic, published influential poetry in all the right places, was reviewed by all the right people, but academic institutions did not continue to teach her, and many of her books fell out of print. Several factors have since combined to move her onto more required reading lists: poet Robert Duncan's *The H.D. Book* (2011), published piecemeal in magazines from the 1960s to 1980s, called attention to her writing among new generations of poets; feminist critics saw her as a natural choice for a modernist woman writer to balance out the male-dominated history of the movement; and Norman Holmes Pearson, a Yale University professor, carefully collected and catalogued H.D.'s literary and personal papers in ways that made her manuscripts easier to publish and to study in depth. Increasingly, H.D. has become a canonical modernist writer.

An even more well-known example explains the pervasive presence of F. Scott Fitzgerald's *The Great Gatsby* in virtually every secondary school in the USA. Originally one of Fitzgerald's less successful novels, *Gatsby* did not even sell out its first printing in 1925. The novel received relatively little attention until after Fitzgerald's death when it was published in 1941 as part of a posthumous volume along with Fitzgerald's final, unfinished novel. In the intervening years, the Great Depression and beginning of World War II made the story of the former World War I army officer far more relevant and its portrayal of the 1920s fodder for economic nostalgia. When *Gatsby* was later selected by the US Armed Service Editions to be sent in paperback format to soldiers around the world, its canonical status was secured.

Part of the strength of the canon, then, lies in its ability to remain fluid, to accommodate new values, new readers, new views. Rather than seeking to 'know' the entire canon at any given time as though it were a fixed and finite set of texts, readers of literature would do better to know the resources that map the shape of the canon. Use the canon to understand the major divisions for categorizing literature – national and regional literatures, major genres, major literary periods – then become familiar with the exemplary texts of each of those categories, while remaining open to change.

READERS, AUTHORS, AND MEANINGS

Literary analysis today recognizes not only that the definition of literature is not objectively fixed but also that the medium of literature – language – does not open a transparent window between author's meanings and readers' minds. Because language functions as a sign system with words acting only as symbols for abstract or concrete objects, meanings can change and multiply in both the surface information being communicated and in the varied ways in which those details are represented (Saussure 1983; Derrida 1982).

Indeed, the assumption that literature is a form of **representation** has guided our understanding of the field for thousands of years. To represent means to portray something or someone; to serve as the substitute or symbol for that object; to signify a concept, place, item, or person through a medium – like words, paint, film, or sculpted marble; and also to present again (*re-present*) an absent or past event or incident. All of these definitions emphasize the gap between the 'real' object of interest, which is now silent, elsewhere, inert, or in the past, and the *representation* of it, the echo, copy, or record of the thing we do not have. When we relate the events of a sports match to a friend who was not there, for instance, we use words to convey the excitement and suspense of a good game. In shifting from the lived experience to its representation in language, however, we lose the possibility of simultaneous sensory stimuli – smelling beer and soda, hearing a shout, feeling the sun, and seeing a play all at the same time. In the previous sentence, I listed the different experiences in quick succession, but the representation simply cannot match the speed of the reality.

Or consider the phenomenon of Madame Tussauds wax museums which have multiplied from the original London site established in 1835 to nearly two dozen locations worldwide. Viewers of these wax representations of famous historical figures and celebrities marvel at the craft necessary to create a sense of verisimilitude (the appearance of being real), but they also note the uncanniness, the unsettling feeling of something that is not quite right about the wax statues which are only *verisimilar*, not true or *veritable*.

In literature, where the places, people, events, and images represented may have no original, 'real' corollary in the world at all, the question of representation is even more complex. In *The Republic* (*c*. 360 BCE), Plato (1992) warned against the ability of literature to create false realities. Noting that literature is a form of *mimesis*, an imitation through representation, Plato worried that readers and audiences could be led morally astray by unvirtuous characters, narratives, and speeches. In contrast, Aristotle's *Poetics* (*c*. 350 BCE) praised the distancing effects of literary representation and imitation. By imitating the nature of the world in what amounts to thought experiments, Aristotle (1997) argued, poets engage in the most instinctive human habits of learning and comprehending through mimicry, impersonation, and play. To use our sports example above, it may well be that revisiting and representing the scene in language, slowing it down, editing it, and savouring it bit-by-bit offer us opportunities for reflection that produce a different kind of pleasure and insight than the 'real', lived event.

Following Aristotle, literary critics today do not view the representative or mimetic characteristics of literature as a mode of deception or source of moral danger. They see literary representation as a major reason that what a text means is not merely the sum of the definitions of its composite words. Therefore, literary analysis is not a summary of plot events or a paraphrase of the dictionary or historical definitions of a poetic line. The meaning exceeds the words on the page and encompasses the larger issues and implicit, unstated connections beneath the surface.

In our daily interactions with language, we have all experienced the multiple meanings that language creates. Clearly, the path from thought to words to meaning can be long and winding. Whether or not we have consciously considered the slippery nature of language, we all know that when we wish to ask a friend a favour, we often begin the conversation on a different, lighter, even flattering topic to make the friend more receptive to the request. We call a car accident a 'fender bender' to reduce anxiety when we tell our family members of the event. And we falter, grasp for language, and knit together strained phrases to express joy, grief, or surprise. We often love, hurt, and appreciate 'more than words can say'. When we do write or speak, the order, tone, diction, juxtapositions, rhythm, speed, formality, and even fluidity or fragmentation of word patterns combine to create several meaning effects that extend far beyond – or even contradict – the surface definitions of the words we use.

How do we identify such meanings through analysis? When we attempt to analyse the meaning of a serious conversation, we take into account several factors:

- reasonable expectations for this particular type of communication, e.g. a job interview, a first date, etc.;
- the words themselves – both their connotations and denotations;
- contextual clues of body language, setting, culture, etc.;
- the previous history of statements made by that person; and
- similarities and differences between this conversation and past conversations with others.

Comparable factors inform our approach to literature. Our analytical strategies begin with studying the words and move outward in ever wider circles of context.

The chapters in this book map the set of contextual factors that experts use to analyse literature. Paralleling the interpretive acts we use in everyday life, literary analysis considers these factors in more specialized terms:

- We categorize the text by *genre* to help us understand the meaning through the common patterns and **convention**s for that particular type of literature (tragedy, comedy, coming-of-age novel, love sonnet, etc.) and its expected readers. (Chapter 2)
- We make careful or *close readings* of the words, identifying stylistic figures and literary forms that may carry additional, nonliteral meanings. (Chapter 2)
- We consider the *context* of other writings by the same author to identify recurrent meanings. (Chapter 3)

- We try to understand the *context* of references and meanings by exploring connections between the literature and major cultural and historical events at the time. (Chapter 3)
- We *compare* the text to other literary texts of the same period and of the past to see whether the meaning runs with or against the grain of other literature. (Chapters 3 and 4)
- We seek other expert opinions about the text by reading *criticism* that may send us on new paths of interpretation. (Chapter 5)
- We identify our underlying assumptions about the nature of literature, culture, and representation and consider alternative *theories* and assumptions that may open up new meanings in the literature we read. (Chapter 6)

It is worth noting here that when it comes to literary analysis, the **author's intentions** do not rank high on this list; the author's experiences and statements more often serve as context for rather than confirmation of meaning. W. K. Wimsatt and Monroe Beardsley (1946, p. 468) famously wrote in 'The Intentional Fallacy', 'the design or intention of the author is neither available nor desirable as a standard for judging the success of a work of literary art'. Their statement remains a central precept of literary analysis today – though not necessarily for the reasons they outlined.

For Wimsatt and Beardsley, the author's intended meaning is 'unavailable' (even if we ask a living author directly about the work) because the act of writing inevitably alters and revises those intentions. In essence, the author's only knowable intention in writing is to produce the best possible work.

Furthermore, even if authors could know and record their more specific intentions at each stage of composition, such lists would not make 'desirable' or valuable contributions to an analysis of the text because the literature produces effects that go beyond the author's intention. For example, Stephenie Meyer's (2008) stated explanation of the origins of *Twilight* begins with a dream and a desire to tell that story in no small part because she was so attracted to the vampire in the scene. Perhaps this explanation suffices for *Twilight* fans who are equally infatuated with the characters, but it does little to aid an analysis of the meaning of a decade-long social and cultural phenomena in print, film, and the Web. Similarly, when J. K. Rowling announced at Carnegie Hall in 2007 that Aldus Dumbledore of the

Harry Potter series was homosexual, her intentions did little to clarify or negate the many rich analyses and interpretations of his character and the series as a whole produced in the ten years prior. According to Wimsatt and Beardsley, the text does what it does – whether it excels or fails to meet the author's intended aims – and the author's intentions are limiting, basic, and even irrelevant to an understanding of a text.

This mid-century criticism paved the way for later scholars to consider the role of an author as distinct from the human who writes. In 'What is an Author?' (1977), Michel Foucault pushed the writer even further from the text by replacing the living author with an 'author-function', constructed through publication practices and criticism to offer a sense of coherence, legitimacy, and authenticity (literally *authority*) to literature. Just like an actor is not a 'star' until after the blockbuster comes out, the author does not exist until readers recognize his or her works. Once the author or star's name achieves that status, it continues to generate power and value in literary or cinematic markets. Publishers will jump at the chance to market a book with the names Salman Rushdie, Stephen King, Kazuo Ishiguro, Cormac McCarthy, or J. K. Rowling printed on the cover, just as film producers do not say no to Sir Ian McKellen, Johnny Depp, or Dame Judi Dench. Other, unknown writers and actors may be equally talented, but the power of well-known names also shapes their texts' meanings (and drives up sales).

J. D. Salinger offers a clear example of the author-function. Jerome Salinger had a complex life as a writer, a soldier, a son, husband, father, and friend – both before and after he published *The Catcher in the Rye* (1951), but once readers met Holden Caulfield, J. D. Salinger, the author-function of the novel, captivated and intrigued readers who thought they knew him and sought him out. Like Romanticists William Wordsworth and Percy Bysshe Shelley who attributed literature solely to the individual genius and inspiration of a great writer, Salinger's fans viewed him as the creator of a character and a world which spoke to the anxieties and disillusionment of generations of readers. Despite the actual Salinger's efforts to resist fans' interpretations of the novel, to pursue different projects and to escape public scrutiny by living in an isolated, rural town, fans and reporters continued to hunt for the embodiment of the public author-function of *The Catcher in the Rye*, and they continued to be disappointed that their authorial fiction did not exist in the real world. For Foucault, the author is not the extraordinary, inspired person who imbues the text with a deliberate meaning. The author-function is society's concept of the person behind the proper name printed on the book; it is another fiction created only when the book is published.

Roland Barthes (1977) goes a step further in his critique of the author, paraphrasing Nietzsche to announce 'The Death of the Author'. For Barthes (1977, p. 143), it is a fallacy to read literature as 'the voice of a single person, the author confiding in us' when both language and ideas inevitably escape the author's control. Focusing on the linguistic materials of literature, Barthes (1977, p. 146) concludes, 'The text is a tissue of quotations drawn from the innumerable centres of culture' and combined by authors much as hip hop artists make mixes and mashups from samples of musical tracks. Literary analysis, then, aims to 'disentangle' texts, not 'decipher' meanings embedded in code by their authors (Barthes 1977, p. 147).

Whether we wish to celebrate the 'death of the author' or attempt to emphasize a sense of the author's power and individual voice, when we perform literary analysis, we must recognize that meanings in literature emerge from a negotiation between readers' interpretations and the texts authors write.

Speaking as part of the Distinguished Writers Series of the Newhouse Center for the Humanities, Colum McCann (2011) admits that much of writing owes itself to a loss of control, noting that when you talk to great writers, 'they say I'm not so sure that I absolutely knew what I was doing, but it happened to me'. Separating the creative act of producing the text from the creation of meaning within it, McCann (2011) explains that readers' interpretations continue to develop both the written text and its author in valuable and essential ways:

> I've seen writers get upset because somebody's taken one of their short stories and as far as they're concerned misinterpreted it. As far as I'm concerned, if somebody gets a meaning out of, say, one of my stories or one of my sentences that's a million miles removed from what I intended, I think all the better.... My little limited world becomes a bigger world because it becomes well-read. So nothing is finished until the reader gets her hands or his hands on it, and then they bring it to a new place. I become infinitely cleverer once people have read a book.

If we, like McCann, adhere to the principles of literary analysis today, we recognize that any intended meanings consciously or unconsciously placed into a text by the author at the time of composition are at best partial clues, at worst red herrings in our efforts to find meaning. The responsibility for making meaning, then, lies firmly with the readers who analyse the texts, not with the writers who often balk at answering questions or turn cagy or coy when asked directly what their works mean.

WHAT DOES IT REALLY MEAN? ANALYSIS AND EVIDENCE

I have written that responsibility for making meaning lies with the readers, but it is important to explain the terms of such a responsibility. Literary analysis is also a public form of meaning-making, designed to contribute to a community of knowledge about literature as a whole and about particular literary texts. The nature of literary representation and language admits multiple possible interpretations, but it does not make literature a textual Rorschach test; the printed, performed, or spoken word cannot be reduced to a metaphorical ink blot open to the infinite free associations of our individual psyches. Thus, as readers, we are empowered to claim the meanings uncovered by our acts of analysis, but we are bound by rules of evidence to ensure the validity of our interpretations.

To return to the analogy of biblical exegesis and hermeneutics, literary analysis also has a theory of interpretation: even in readings that draw from context, criticism, and **literary theory**, meanings and interpretations must also be supported by evidence from the text. Another term from religious scholarship may explain this distinction. Theologians are repeatedly warned against what is called *eisegesis*, exegesis's opposite, in which the reader begins with a set of assumptions and values then finds evidence of them ('reads into') in the text being studied. With sacred texts where ultimate spiritual authority lies within the printed page, all critical explanation must begin with the words; eisegesis can, therefore, amount to blasphemy.

The penalties for eisegesis or reading into *literary* texts during analysis are much less extreme, but the principle still holds. Any reading that begins with readers' own experiences and views of the world in general then seeks confirmation of these in the text is invalid as literary analysis. For example, a faulty literary analysis might summarize the story of a literary character – Jay Gatsby's drive towards class mobility or Daisy's inconstant commitment to the two men she claims to 'love' – then note how 'true' that story is because the same things happen today. They do, but it is not literary analysis to say so.

A better analogy for the process of literary analysis is detective work. In detective fiction or real-world casework, the detective is given a text – the scene of a crime, the notice of a missing person. The initial scene is merely the surface of a much fuller story whose meaning is not yet understood. The detective then breaks the scene apart, carefully examining each detail and seeking more contextual information in order to uncover the meanings – motivations, consequences, even conclusions about human behaviour or the nature of justice – within the case.

Detectives who bring their own set of assumptions to the case can see only what their prejudgements allow them to notice; they may waste a great deal of time pursuing false leads because they are sure that the husband always murders the wife, the estranged parent always kidnaps the child, the scholarship kid always steals from the school, and the butler always does it. Detectives who reason from the available evidence, however, can follow a path towards meaning that will account for everything within the scene. This is the method of Sir Arthur Conan Doyle's Sherlock Holmes (1887) and Agatha Christie's Miss Marple (1930) and Hercule Poirot (1920).

For readers, the text is our mystery to solve, and the words themselves serve as the primary basis for our evidence. We analyse by tracing the patterns among the words, following them back to their audiences and their cultural and historical contexts, and uncovering the connections between them and other texts.

The meanings we find through careful analysis allow us to recognize the depth of knowledge, insight, and revolution embodied within literature. Such analysis does not dampen our initial aesthetic and emotional pleasures in reading, but deepens them by opening up new avenues to understand the causes of that pleasure and to share our interpretations with others. Our shared acts of literary analysis stimulate fresh comparisons and connections that bring the meaning of the literature to life again in new cultures and times.

REFERENCES AND FURTHER READING

Aristotle (1997) *Poetics*, trans. M. Heath, New York: Penguin.

Arnold, M. (1869) *Culture and Anarchy: An Essay in Political and Social Criticism*, London: Smith, Elder, and Co.

Barnes, J. (2012) '"Posterity is Dispossessed": Laurence Olivier's *Macbeth* Manuscripts in 1958 and 2012', *Shakespeare Bulletin*, vol. 30, no. 3, pp. 263–297.

Barthes, R. (1977) 'The Death of the Author', in S. Heath (trans. and ed.), *Image-Music-Text*, New York: Hill & Wang.

Bloom, H. (2001) *How to Read and Why*, New York: Touchstone.

Christie, A. (1920) *The Mysterious Affair at Styles*, New York: John Lane.

Christie, A. (1930) *The Murder at the Vicarage*, London: Collins Crime Club.

Derrida, J. (1982) *Margins of Philosophy*, trans. A. Bass, Chicago: University of Chicago Press.

Doyle, A. C. (1887) *A Study in Scarlet*, London: Ward Lock and Co.

Duncan, R. (2011) *The H.D. Book*, ed. M. Boughn and V. Coleman, Berkeley: University of California Press.

Eagleton, T. (2008) *Literary Theory: An Introduction*, anniversary ed., Oxford: Blackwell.

Felski, R. (2008) *Uses of Literature*, Oxford: Blackwell.

Fiedler, L. A., and Baker, H. A. (eds.) (1981) *English Literature: Opening Up the Canon*, Baltimore, MD: Johns Hopkins University Press.

Foucault, M. (1977) *Language, Counter-Memory Practice: Selected Essays and Interviews*, ed. D. F. Bouchard, New York: Cornell University Press.

Gilbert, S., and Gubar, S. (1979) *The Madwoman in the Attic*, New Haven, CT: Yale University Press.

Gilbert, S., and Gubar, S. (1988, 1994) *No Man's Land: The Place of the Woman Writer in the Twentieth Century*, vols. 1–3, New Haven, CT: Yale University Press.

Graff, G. (2007) *Professing Literature: An Institutional History*, 20th anniversary ed., Chicago: University of Chicago Press.

Guillory, J. (1993) *Cultural Capital: The Problem of Literary Canon Formation*, Chicago: University of Chicago Press.

Kermode, F. (1989) *History and Value: The Clarendon Lectures and the Northcliffe Lectures 1987*, Oxford: Oxford University Press.

McCann, C. (2011) Colum McCann reads *Let the Great World Spin*. Newhouse Center for the Humanities [Podcast]. 9 Feb. Available online: https://itunes.apple.com/us/itunes-u/newhouse-center-for-humanities/id419327844?mt=10 (accessed 20 May 2015).

Meyer, S. (2008) *The Twilight Saga Collection*, New York and Boston: Little, Brown.

Plato (1992) *The Republic*, trans. G. M. A. Grube, Indianapolis and Cambridge, MA: Hackett.

Salinger, J. D. (1951) *The Catcher in the Rye*, Boston: Little, Brown.

Saussure, F. (1983) *Course in General Linguistics*, trans. R. Harris, London: Duckworth.

Shakespeare, W. (2008) *The Tragedy of Macbeth*, ed. Nicholas Brooke, Oxford: Oxford University Press.

Williams, R. (1976) *Keywords: A Vocabulary of Culture and Society*, New York: Oxford University Press.

Wimsatt, W. K., and Beardsley, M. C. (1946) 'The Intentional Fallacy', *The Sewanee Review*, vol. 54, no. 3, pp. 468–488.

Woolf, V. (1981) *A Room of One's Own*, New York: Harcourt Brace Jovanovich.

CLOSE READING: WORDS AND FORMS

If we consider the process of literary analysis in everyday practice, we see that readers most often approach literature by selecting and categorizing a **text** – both as **canonical** or non-canonical (see Chapter 1, 'Introduction: thinking about literature'), and as an example of the **genre** or type of literature to which it belongs. In most digital film, book, or music stores, genre categories define the entire search and selection process. In brick-and-mortar bookstores, readers may bypass the shelves of popular new releases with glossy photos from film adaptations in favour of the shocking, bold fonts of crime novels, or the jewel tones and elaborate costumes on the covers of fantasy and science fiction. Or perhaps readers march straight to the back of the store, to the darker, more staid covers of fiction **classic**s in blacks, greys, and golds.

After establishing a foundation for their literary experience through first impressions based on genre, readers proceed to the words on the page and begin to explore the way language and structure shape the overall meaning. These analytical strategies apply equally to poetry and film, tragic theatre and animated cartoons, classical masterpieces, and beach reads.

This chapter outlines the way to analyse texts using the technique of close reading and careful attention to the specialized genres, forms, and **figures of speech** that enable the text to generate its meanings and effects.

ANIMAL, VEGETABLE, OR MINERAL:
WHY GENRE MATTERS

Genres and subgenres are to literature what genus and species are to biology, and the value of identifying genre or genus is about the same. Spotting a member of the *Ursus* genus in the distance while on a hike conveys valuable information long before the hiker gets close enough to meet that particular bear. Knowing the genus allows the hiker to identify typical characteristics – large teeth and claws, for instance – and to predict common behaviours, such as hunting prey. The same is true of genre in literature.

Even before we begin reading any text, its basic formal features send us down a specific analytical path. Our ability to categorize texts quickly and even subconsciously allows us to associate them with clearly defined patterns of structure and meaning-making. In the age of television, audiences can classify genre based on theme song, station, time of broadcast, set design, lighting, and even the title font. If characters are lounging on sofas or sharing a meal in the opening credits, viewers can expect a situation comedy with minor domestic troubles neatly resolved through a combination of slapstick and wit in 30 minutes or less.

In literature, the first formal features that signify genre include text length, internal divisions (e.g. chapters, acts, scenes, stories, essays, or poems), distribution of white space and line or paragraph spacing on the page, and inclusion of introductory material or notes within the text (e.g. epigraph, dramatis personae, author's prologue or preface, footnotes, or references). When we choose to read any text, from a two-paragraph online movie review to the more than 1,200-page novel *War and Peace* (1869), we use clues of formatting to classify the text and guide us through strategies for reading it. When we discuss genre, then, we refer to the pattern of formal and structural elements a text follows and the expectations that such forms set up for readers.

If we select a mystery, we expect the action to unwind slowly with central plot elements withheld until the very end. The suspense of not knowing the truth about some characters or events keeps readers eagerly turning pages while hunting for details in a race to solve the mystery before the characters do.

Choosing a love sonnet or a *lyric* poem, however, creates an entirely different set of reading expectations. In the stereotypical lyric, a speaker expresses emotions through **figurative** uses of language that make those feelings come vividly to life. In reading such poems, we slow down, pay attention to each word and sound, and anticipate that the meaning will emerge through the progress of the speaker's reflections across the lines. More importantly, we expect that the intimate, personal contemplations of this poetic speaker will in some way resonate with broader human experience and articulate a collective human truth. We do not read the lines as self-centred or self-indulgent; we seek in them a glimpse of the profound and sublime. In his book about genre, author John Frow (2006, p. 19) studies the ways in which genres 'create effects of reality and truth' by calling readers to observe the 'effects of authority and plausibility which are specific to the genre'. In the love sonnet or lyric, the speaker's emotions shape the reality of the poem, giving emotion itself a kind of authority within the poem.

As the examples above suggest, there are both large and small categories for classifying texts. In *The Republic* (*c.* 360 BCE), Plato (1992) divided literature into **narrative**, mimetic/dramatic, and mixed (e.g. epic) forms, though in his time and culture all three types were written in **verse**, not **prose**. Both those classifications and our interpretations of them have changed over the history of literary **criticism** (see Genette 1992, Duff 2000). Generally speaking, we can think of drama, poetry, and prose as the most significant genres into which literature is divided today. Yet that list is also subject to revision. With ongoing innovations in digital and multimedia literary forms, the list of major genres will surely continue to change in the future as well.

DRAMA

Perhaps the simplest literary genre to identify, drama uses actors to perform the dialogue and actions of the characters whose stories are being told. Beyond the words on the page, the play incorporates the stage set and set design, the costumes, and the very bodies and voices of the actors. Although the published play or screenplay may include detailed character descriptions or backgrounds, stage directions to announce entrances, exits, and other movements, or even commentary on costumes and set design, readers and performers recognize that only the lines of dialogue attributed to characters are meant to be voiced aloud. Produced collaboratively with the playwright or screenwriter, director, actors, and behind-the-scenes contributors, drama creates a physical world in which readers and audiences can participate with all their senses.

POETRY

Poet and critic Donald Hall (1993, p. 1) has evocatively called poetry 'pleasure first, bodily pleasure, a deliciousness of the senses', adding that by the end most poems say 'something (even the unsayable)'. To view poetry in more concrete terms, readers will note that the visual impact of poetry on the page is one of gaps and spaces. Most commonly – though not always – poetry is written in *verse*, meaning that words are grouped and divided purposely, not allowed to flow naturally across the margins of the page. Because poets exploit the breaks between words and lines as well as the arrangement of words within sentences or phrases, poetry may be likened to music, which was an essential part of its historical roots. As with music, often patterns of rhythm and rhyme lend poetry an important aural component, though neither a regular beat nor repeating rhyme is required.

Individual poems may be quite short or extend across dozens of pages, and it is important to note that verse plays, such as Johann Wolfgang von Goethe's *Faust* (1808), and epic poems, like Homer's *Odyssey* (*c.* 800 BCE), are comparable in length to texts in any other genre.

Conventionally, we call the 'voice' of the poem the speaker, regardless of whether that person seems to be nearly identical to the poet or an invented character or *persona* speaking dialogue or sharing an interior reflection.

PROSE

While we are often tempted to assume that prose refers to a novel due to the dominance of that literary form today, the genre of prose actually covers nearly everything that is not poetry or drama. Its distinguishing visual feature is the presence of paragraphs running steadily down the page. Prose writers do not manipulate individual line breaks and word placement, nor do they expect their characters' words to be spoken and performed, but otherwise the content, purpose, length, and internal divisions of the text are completely open to the writer.

Prose can depict invented people, places, and events as in *fictional* short stories or novels, or it can be *nonfictional* as in literary essays, biographies, memoirs, or histories. Creative non-fiction essays, letters, and speeches about any number of subjects were the first prose literary forms. In English literary history, sketches, stories, and vignettes appeared next, followed only in the eighteenth-century by the *novel*. The English novel emerged out of medieval French *romans*, the chivalric romances of knights and ladies written in prose as early as the thirteenth century. The later influence of the Spanish *Don Quixote* (1605) brought more middle-class concerns to the developing form. Aphra Behn's *Oroonoko* (1688) and Daniel Defoe's *Robinson Crusoe* (1719) are often considered the first novels in English. Both relate adventure stories of travellers to the New World through first-person narrators who make every effort to portray their stories as true reports of real, living people, yet both are fictional narratives, and Defoe never even visited the Americas. Increasingly, semiautobiographical fiction, historical fiction, New Journalism in which personal and creative narratives blend with conventional reporting, metafiction in which the **author** intrudes upon the fictional text to discuss the limits or process of writing, and other prose forms have blurred the distinction between fiction and nonfiction.

In prose, we usually refer to the 'voice' imagined to be speaking the words on the page as the narrator. Like the speaker in poetry, the narrator may be clearly designated as a character or may be a disembodied figure who may or may not be similar to the author.

GENERIC CONVENTION

Each major genre comprises several more specific subgenres, including novels, short stories, historiographic metafiction, nonfiction prose essays, autobiography, tragedy, comedy, history plays, passion plays, musicals, horror films, epic poetry, lyric poetry, sonnets, elegies, ballads, and many more. The genre or subgenre helps to convey the rules for reading and conventions for writing that govern the style and content the author may present. In *Genre*, Heather Dubrow (1982) likens **generic convention**s to rules of etiquette and other shared codes for social behaviour.

See a *tragedy* expecting an adventure story and you may be distressed and even disturbed by the way the most sympathetic characters and heroes are destroyed in the end. Aristotle's *Poetics* (1997, p. 21) describes the dramatic tragedy as driven by the actions of characters who are above the norm, yet flawed, whose reversal of fortune when they recognize their errors too late elicits pity and fear. Witnessing the loss and fall of the tragic figure leads to a catharsis or venting of the audience's emotions as the audience realizes they have escaped that tragic fate, but the dominant experience remains sorrowful. In contrast, the adventure genre plays on adrenalin and suspense released in the end by a return to safety and confidence or optimism that tragedy cannot provide.

Likewise, if you pick up an autobiography expecting a *comedy*, you will be deeply disappointed by the self-absorption of the main character. Displaying a general sense of play and joy despite challenges, a *comedy* requires a happy ending and rise in fortune for the main characters who start their story with room to improve their status (e.g. William Shakespeare's *The Taming of the Shrew* or *Much Ado About Nothing*, both written in the 1590s). While *The Autobiography of Benjamin Franklin* (1791) may be amusing at times, its aim as autobiography should always be to convey the experience of a singular life, generally in chronological order with the benefit of hindsight guiding the selection of significant scenes and events. The conventions of autobiography dictate that telling a true, nonfiction, first-person account of a life must be more important than maintaining an upbeat and even humorous style.

Despite the comfort of having expectations fulfilled by texts that behave the way their genres predict, readers often reject texts that follow the rules of genre too closely. Texts which obey all generic conventions to the letter become predictable and formulaic – in a word, boring. Often writers achieve innovation and originality only by bending, questioning, or even breaking expectations of genre. Indeed, in 'The Origin of Genres', Tzvetan Todorov (1976, p. 159) notes that 'the authentically modern writer . . . no longer respects the separation of genres', in much the same way that many contemporary societies no longer 'respect' traditional divisions that were so important to social institutions of the past. After centuries of experimentation *within* genres, some of the most creative literature today works *across* genres in order to shape the genres that will come to dominate future generations.

Carolyn Forché's 'The Colonel,' for instance, offers a clear example of a text that employs and exploits several genres at once. Published in Forché's 1981 poetry collection, *The Country Between Us*, 'The Colonel' is ostensibly a poem, but its wide block format, spreading from margin to margin with no breaks for lines or *stanzas* (groups of lines with a blank line following), already makes it a generic hybrid – a *prose poem*. Within the poem, the speaker at first adopts the objectively straightforward voice of a reporter or a witness at a trial as she describes a visit to the home of a military leader during the Salvadoran Civil War. The poem is, in fact, based upon Forché's work in El Salvador as a human rights activist and Guggenheim Fellow researching for her poetry collection; therefore, the incorporation of a nonfiction prose genre certainly fits the content. However, as the prose poem draws to a close, the tightly-controlled language begins to break down. Abandoning quotation marks around the colonel's dialogue and blending poetic images of the signs of his war-time atrocities with the speaker's stunned reluctance to continue to describe the horrific scene of trophies from his torture victims, the poem breaks many rules and resists any single classification. In many ways, its point is the inadequacy of language to bear witness to acts of human cruelty. And the poem makes that point by tearing at genre's seams.

For many contemporary critics and writers, pushing the boundaries of genre is simply part of the nature of generic categories. **Literary theorist** Jacques Derrida (1980, p. 212) writes in 'The Law of Genre' that texts do not *belong* to a genre, they *participate* in at least one genre. In this way, Derrida suggests that genre does not include or exclude texts in the way a family would welcome children and spouses but expel strangers from its rigid borders. Instead, genre offers up practices or rituals that demonstrate commonalities, and texts may engage in practices from a range of genres all at once. Most importantly, each time a text sends up the signal of a particular genre – even mocking it – it redefines the genre in slightly new ways.

For example, former US Poet Laureate Rita Dove comments on the power of the sonnet genre both to structure poetry and to entrap it. Throughout *Mother Love*, Dove (1995) writes variations on the *sonnet* – 14 lines long with ten-syllable lines, and one of two standard rhyme structures – but her poems rarely follow an iambic pentameter rhythm, hardly ever employ a rhyming pattern, seldom use the stanza divisions typical of Petrarch's or Shakespeare's sonnets, and never elevate the language to mask the rawness or pain of the acts of love at the heart of the collection. Writing of the myth of Demeter, Persephone, and Hades, Dove makes Hades a slick-talking seducer living in Paris who brings Persephone a drink at a party. Poems like 'Hades' Pitch' or 'Demeter, Waiting' bluntly describe erotic attraction and maternal devotion. A bored exchange student, Persephone finds herself attracted to Hades precisely because he does not offer a safe relationship (Dove 1995, p. 37). The long-distance mother, Demeter vows to rage against the loss of her daughter until she gives up in self-loathing and simply waits for her to return (Dove 1995, p. 56). The emotional power and psychological revelations of the poems are clear. Reading them through the expectations and conventions of the sonnet genre, however, adds new contrast between their stark reality and the tight and beautiful rhymes of love sonnets of the past. Dove uses a centuries-old, traditional form for writing about love in order to show that we may not know as much about love (or about poetry) as we thought we did.

Yet Dove does not see her work as a 'violation' of the sonnet form. She notes, 'I will simply say that I like how the sonnet comforts even while its prim borders (but what a pretty fence!) are stultifying; one is constantly bumping up against Order' (Dove 1995, foreword). Today's critics and writers increasingly analyse genre in the collision between the individual text and the conventions of the genre or genres the text explores. As a result, meaning comes not only from the text's content but also from the strategies it uses for fitting that content into a particular genre or genres and into the functions those genres are expected to serve.

ANALYSING LANGUAGE

While genre provides a good orientation to any work of literature, literary analysis depends upon reading and interpreting the individual words of a text. Here *reading* means not only understanding the surface meaning of the sentences, but comprehending the deep underlying meanings within and connections among them.

In *Practical Criticism*, I. A. Richards (1930, p. 13) describes the initial surface reading as making out the text's 'plain, overt meaning, as a set of ordinary intelligible, English sentences'. Surface readings find the literal definitions (*denotations*) of the words and use grammar cues to determine the relationships among them. Approaching the sentence, 'Soft fell the snow', the plain reader notes the sentence subject (snow) and verb (fell) and concludes that the sentence means that the snow fell softly, not with a harsh or fast whipping of winds.

Such readings are necessary to enable interpretation of a text, but they fall far short of literary analysis. Analysis demands that readers break apart the text into its details to determine how they work and why they work that way. For critic John Guillory (2008, p. 9), analysis and interpretation are complex and creative processes: 'By *interpretation* I mean the capacity of a reader to re-understand the words of a text by translating these words into a new frame of reference'. With this model, readers assume that the text says far more than its literal meaning and that the particular way the text adds feelings or undertones (*connotations*) to the words and forges connections across its different parts creates meanings and insights that the basic definitions of words alone cannot convey. The positive and gentle connotations of 'soft' at the beginning of the sentence 'Soft fell the snow', for instance, evoke a tenderness and perhaps even nostalgia that imply an emotional content much deeper than a simple weather report.

In a more thorough example, reading F. Scott Fitzgerald's *The Great Gatsby* (1925) literally might suggest that is about Jay Gatsby's attempt to reconnect with Daisy Buchanan, his lost love. By reading deeply and interpreting, however, we see that Gatsby associates Daisy not so much with love as with money and the freedom that wealth and social status provide. He does not want to return to the past as much as he wants to rewrite his past as Daisy's social equal. Looking at the text through a new frame of reference – for instance focused on its word choices that emphasize characters' different ethnic names, immigrant heritages, and American regional backgrounds – interpreters of *The Great Gatsby* see that Tom Buchanan's discussion of white supremacist texts over dinner, the African American witness to the car accident, and even narrator Nick Carraway's focus on the American West all connect together to explain the impossibility of Gatsby's (aka James 'Jimmy' Gatz) dreams.

In literary analysis, the method of interpreting the detailed use of language is called ***close reading***. Despite many changes in the field of literary studies, since the early twentieth century, close reading has served as the cornerstone of literary analysis. First developed in the late 1920s and early 1930s by the British scholars of Practical Criticism and the American New Critics, close reading demanded that critics focus their attention on the text alone, using detailed etymologies of words to identify multiple meanings within lines, then exploring the ways that the beauty of the text as a whole held together its complex meanings. Practical Criticism and New Criticism brought literary study into the university system as 'serious criticism' (Green 2012, p. 65), founded on sound, objective intellectual principles rooted exclusively in the words on the page, not on the reader's personal, subjective responses or even the social significance of the text's content.

Although both personal and social or political responses have again become a part of literary analysis, in 'Close Reading in 2009', Jane Gallop (2010, p. 15) argues that close reading is 'the most valuable thing English ever had to offer' and 'the very thing that made us a discipline, that transformed us from cultured gentlemen into a profession'. Despite the burgeoning of digital humanities approaches to technology-based, bulk textual analysis and abstract model-building (Moretti 2013) or increasing attention to affectively focused, 'uncritical' responses (Warner 2004), critic Daniel Green (2012, p. 70) notes that even newer schools of literary criticism and analysis that seem to oppose New Criticism 'really only do so by affirming an underlying premise held in common', often the premise of close reading. I would further emphasize that the majority of experts who currently advocate alternative strategies to literary analysis have already cemented their reputations by mastering basic close reading techniques.

An important advocate of New Criticism in the mid-twentieth century, Reuben Brower (1951), describes the method of close reading as a slow examination of a text, reading and re-reading multiple times to ensure that every detail has been explored. As a professor at Harvard University in the 1950s, Brower taught students to select a single detail, even a single word, and trace the many connections that could be found throughout the text. Working predominantly with poetry due to the intensity of the task, Brower (1951, p. 8) analysed the relationships among words based on grammar, logic, imagery, metaphor, rhythm, sound, and dramatic intensity. Thus, close reading considers each word horizontally as it relates to the other words and sentences around it and vertically as it relates to the history and development of the word's meaning.

Is such close reading necessary? Absolutely. Because art, logic, imagination, the senses, history, culture, and psychology all meet in literature, we cannot treat it as mere communication. For New Critics like Cleanth Brooks, literature communicates on multiple levels at once. Writing about poetry, Brooks (1975, p. 73) states, 'The poem communicates so much and communicates it so richly and with such delicate qualifications that the thing communicated is mauled and distorted if we attempt to convey it by any vehicle less subtle that that of the poem itself'. Here he argues that the details of the poem are not merely decorations flowering over a rather straightforward idea; instead, the images, metaphors, sounds, rhythms, and other artistic elements express complex, interrelated concepts. The same holds true for any kind of literature, and close readings can be applied to any text – from political speeches to advertisements or even conversations with friends.

HOW TO MAKE A CLOSE READING

First, select a text and, as Richards suggests, read once to understand the basic, surface-level plot and grammatical meaning of the sentences and words. Read any particularly interesting or difficult passages aloud to hear the rhythm and tone of the language. Look up definitions of any unknown words. Identify the speaker or narrator: is he or she a particular character or persona, a person from a particular time or culture, or an unnamed figure observing or reflecting within the text? Consider any details of setting or **context**, including the time period, location, and social conditions. Make note of the publication date and any differences between it and the time period described within the text. For example, Mark Twain's *Adventures of Huckleberry Finn* (1885) was published two decades after the abolition of slavery in the USA, but the plot takes place in roughly the 1830s in slave states of the American South. The narrator is Huck himself, a poor white boy whose friendship with the wealthier Tom Sawyer has given him an unusual position in the community. These basic details, the facts of the text, will be necessary to complete a close reading.

To begin close reading, select a particular passage or segment of a text and answer the following questions:

- What is the *general topic* of the passage as compared to that of the text as a whole? Also consider the title or *epigraph* (introductory quote after the title) as indicators of topic when doing a close reading of the beginning of a text. This topic may differ from the surface idea or event being discussed as the word choices in the passage draw attention to multiple, deeper layers of ideas. For example, as Nick Carraway lists the dozens of party goers in *The Great Gatsby*, the repetition of ethnic names, occupations, infidelities and crimes makes the scene a portrait of American culture in transition or crisis, not merely idle party gossip.

- What are the *major images, metaphors, or literary figures* in the passage? Which images, words, sounds, or ideas recur and relate literally, physically, or through their underlying connotations? How do these images or **literary figure**s (many listed under 'Poetics and literary terms' below) relate to the general topic? Do they support, contradict, or provide a subtext for the general topic? Descriptions of cars pervade *The Great Gatsby*. Their fast, sleek, expensive, and modern bodies are always teetering on the edge of disaster as a sign of the out-of-control lives of their drivers.

- How do the *characteristics, tone, and social position of the speaker or narrator* affect the meaning of the passage? Should we believe what the speaker or narrator says, or should we be sceptical? Does a seemingly straightforward tone hint at *satire* or sarcasm? In satire, the text may appear to be serious, but may offer outrageous or comical statements that clearly criticize any real society that behaves in the way its fictional settings are described (e.g. *Adventures of Huckleberry Finn* or Jonathan Swift's 1726 novel *Gulliver's Travels*). As the narrator of *The Great Gatsby*, Nick Carraway is not satirical, yet it is still wise to remain suspicious about his observations. He tells us that he is an open-minded person who avoids criticizing those around him, but in the same sentence, he also notes that many dull and unusual characters have consequently told him their stories (Fitzgerald 1925, p.1). Is he reserving judgement or is he such a bad judge of his own character that he does not see how judgemental he really is? Can we trust him to give accurate accounts of other characters if he so misjudges himself?

- How does the *form* of the passage affect the meaning? Does the form fit genre conventions or is it experimental? Is it regular or more erratic? Does the form make it easier or more difficult to read? How does the form and its ease or difficulty relate to the main ideas of the text? For instance, why does it take so long for Nick to describe Gatsby in the novel named for him? How does the wait for the title character add to our understanding of Gatsby's attempts to create an upper-class identity?
- Finally, how does this *passage fit in with the rest of the text*? Is it consistent or does it make a surprising reversal? If there is a reversal, what does that say about the text's overall meaning? The best known image in *The Great Gatsby* is undoubtedly the billboard advertisement for Doctor T. J. Eckleburg, featuring only the eyes floating behind yellow glasses. Readers may be tempted to interpret these watchful eyes as an omniscient god, as the poor character George Wilson does, but that concept of divine purpose, meaning, or morality conflicts with the overwhelmingly meaningless and amoral events and images of the rest of the text. God is not a subtext for Gatsby's efforts to climb the social ladder. Instead, if we close read the entire image surrounding the eyes, the abandoned billboard and missing facial details contribute to the impression of lost identity and instability experienced by both Gatsby and Nick.

Now we will put these questions to work on a single passage in James Joyce's short story 'The Dead' (1914). In it, two Irish characters, Gabriel Conroy and Miss Ivors, discuss why Gabriel secretly publishes unsigned book reviews in a pro-British paper. Following only Gabriel's train of thought, this conversation seems to be merely about whether or not book reviews can be apolitical if published in a political press.

However, the surface level is only part of what is going on. The whole conversation takes place during a dance, and the text constantly interrupts the dialogue with spins and twirls and dance moves whose names hint at the deep disagreement between the dancers. The main topic of the passage, however, is neither book reviews, nor dancing; a close reading reveals that the scene depicts a struggle to understand Irish identity.

Joyce's description of the folkdance uses the double-meaning of its name, the 'lancers', to evoke a battle as the dancers cross and chain together. The words of the passage focus on surrenders, concessions, and retreats in order to convey Gabriel's sense of being attacked. With each part of the dance, the conversation begins anew, warmly and often with smiles, as the dancers' hands meet, but their political disagreements melt the smiles and divide them just as quickly as the dance does. Throughout the passage, Gabriel's mind seems to be spinning along with his body as Miss Ivors forces him to question his intellectual ability and to admit to preferring Europe over Ireland.

A literary analysis of the scene must interpret why those two, different elements (dance and conversation) are narrated together and what effect the dance has on the meaning and value of the conversation. Plotting the language used to describe the dance steps alongside the verbal argument reveals that Miss Ivors's accusations of anti-Irish sentiment shake Gabriel's identity to the core. A close reading of word choices, violent military imagery, and the interplay between dialogue and description suggests that the violence of the early-1900s Irish independence movement simmers beneath every aspect of the characters' everyday lives.

Ultimately, close readings must pay careful attention to the text's particular words and patterns of language in order to interpret the additional layers of meaning beyond the logic of the words' dictionary definitions. At the level of definition, the film title *Military Conflict in Space* would mean the same thing as *Star Wars* (1977), but the rhyme and repetition in the latter title make it more inspiring, more epic, and more literary. Arnold Schwarzenegger's robot character in *The Terminator* movies (1984) could have said, 'I'll see you again', but the phrase takes on the double menace of a threat and a promise when he says, 'I'll be back'. Likewise, Shakespeare could have called his 1611 play *The Big Storm*, but *The Tempest* hints at the psychological and interpersonal levels of chaos and turmoil that accompany the weather in the play. Ezra Pound could have used the title 'In a Subway Station', but 'In a Station of the Metro' (1913) not only confirms the setting in Paris but also evokes the stillness of the stationary, waiting area within the rushing underground train system. The title phrase also uses an uncommon word order to remind readers of the French *la station de metro*, suggesting that the poem is in part a translation of the experience. At the heart of literary analysis, then, lies an intense awareness of language and the relationships between words and forms.

POETICS AND LITERARY TERMS

As noted above, literature is a mode of communication, but one deeply concerned with aesthetics as well. In philosophy, aesthetics is the study of beauty and art, but in its broader definition, the term derives from the Greek word for perceiving, sensing, and feeling. Education scholar Sir Ken Robinson emphasizes the function of aesthetics in contrast to the numbing, paralyzing qualities of anaesthesia: 'An aesthetic experience is one in which your senses are operating at their peak; when you're present in the current moment; when you're resonating with the excitement of this thing that you're experiencing; when you're fully alive' (2008). In literature, the aesthetic experience is constructed almost entirely of language as writers deploy the physical sounds of spoken words, their visual appearance on the page, as well as their ability to evoke other sensory and emotional content to create a lived experience in readers.

The study of poetics catalogues and names the vast set of literary strategies for producing such effects through literature of all sorts, not just poetry. In the early twentieth century, in particular, schools of literary scholars called formalists and structuralists sought to identify what gave language the power to evoke an aesthetic experience by studying literary structures, forms, and figures of speech. In 1917, Russian formalist Viktor Shklovsky (1965, p. 22) described that power as *defamiliarization*, the process of artistic creation designed to 'remove the automatism of perception', a mechanical way of taking in words and meanings without perceiving the ideas and images that may once have seemed fresh and new. The cliché 'slow as a snail', for example, is too familiar; it no longer evokes vivid mental images of a persistent snail oozing its way without legs or arms along the sidewalk. Yet when we 'defamiliarize' the phrase by calling to mind the courageous drive of the legless creature, propelling itself and its heavy shell seemingly by sheer force of will, we shift our focus and begin to perceive in a new way.

The literary techniques of defamiliarization use new combinations and connections among words in order to prevent readers from taking language for granted and to force them into awareness of the full sensory and intellectual details of the text.

Writers defamiliarize by using strategies, structures, and forms that cause readers to slow down and experience the language aesthetically, not merely functionally.

Literary scholars have identified myriad terms for such strategies, structures, and forms, and these specialized terms allow readers to describe clearly and concisely the effects they encounter in close readings. Listing every important literary term goes far beyond the scope of this basic introduction to literary analysis, but readers should be aware of the many comprehensive guides to literary terms to assist with further study (see Abrahms and Harpham 2014, Greene 2012). The sections below highlight some of the most common literary terms, including terms for some genres, literary styles, figures of speech, and overall structures. These are divided into two categories: 'Structures and forms' describes those literary strategies that determine the text's entire, global pattern; 'Figurative language and textual tactics' illustrates some of the effects created within particular lines, passages, or sections.

STRUCTURES AND FORMS

Perhaps one of the most important literary structures is *narrative*, the umbrella term for the sequence of actions related in a text. Poems, plays, fiction, biography, even 30-second television commercials may all use a narrative arc to unfold events experienced by some characters or actors. In 'An Introduction to the Structural Analysis of Narrative', Roland Barthes (1975, p. 237) links narrative with a sequential logic that can be found in 'myth, legend, fables, tales, short stories, epics, history, tragedy, *drame*, comedy, pantomine, paintings (in *The Legend of Santa Ursula* by Carpaccio, for instance), stained-glass windows, movies, local news, conversation'.

As anyone who has seen Sophocles' play *Oedipus the King* (*c.* 420 BCE), read Homer's *The Odyssey*, or watched the film adaptation of Chuck Palahniuk's *Fight Club* (1996) can attest, narrative includes more than a chronological relation of events. It is the way the story is told and the choice of which events to divulge and which to withhold, which to speed through and which to slow down, which to progress towards and which to *flashback* to in memory, that make the *plot* of a narrative (Genette 1980). If Sophocles had told the story of Oedipus mechanically from his birth amid incestuous and murderous prophesies to his adoption by a neighbouring king, the accidental slaying of his birth father, marriage to his birth mother, and later realization of these realities, the play would lack any surprise, suspense, or interest. Because we discover these events through Oedipus's own innocent investigation into the murder of King Laius (his birth father), the tragedy of Oedipus's family's fate leaves readers cursing the prophesies that sent Oedipus out to avoid killing his father in the first place.

In studies of narrative structure, Russian Formalist scholars distinguished between the basic, unadorned events (the *fabula* or story) and the plot (or what they called the *szužet*) which unfolds in patterns designed to create aesthetic and dramatic effects through the strategies of storytelling employed by a *narrator* (Erlich 1980, p. 242). Applied to an auction, the *fabula* lists the basic facts of the asking price and the final sale, the *plot* comes out through the auctioneer's chant that lures bidders with the excitement of competition, suspense, and reward. Whether the narrator is identified with the author – as in Dante's telling of his seemingly personal journey through hell in the poetry of *Inferno* (*c.* 1308–1314) – or with a fictional figure participating in the plot of the narrative – as in Herman Melville's Ishmael who is a sailor on the whale hunt in *Moby Dick* (1851) – the narrator shapes the story into a plot by selecting which details to relate in which order.

Acting almost as a camera lens made of words, the narrator determines whether we view a scene broadly in a description of the landscape or historical background or whether we zoom in on minute details of emotion or even interior thoughts of a character. Indeed, the issue of lens or perspective is a defining characteristic of a narrator, and literary studies distinguish between different types of narrators based on what has traditionally been called the point of view, including the narrative level, the mode of narration, and the voice. Most narratives written in the third person describe the events that happen to characters ('him' or 'her') from a heterodiegetic position external to the characters within the narrative, but their voice may describe events at a variety of different narrative levels – as wholly external observers, as members of the same world being narrated but separate from the characters' lives, or as narrators of a story within a story (Genette 1980, pp. 228–9). In many narratives, the narrators shift among these different levels throughout the course of the text.

Narrators whose voices speak in the first person as an 'I' reveal to readers their own observations and conclusions about the actions in the texts. Structuralist Gérard Genette (1980, p. 245) calls such narrators homodiegetic, meaning that they are as present within the world created in the narrative as any of the other characters, though Genette distinguishes between those first-person narrators who are the heroes of the stories they tell (autodiegetic) and those who play more marginal roles within the text. Nick Carraway tells Gatsby's story in the first-person as a character who often participates in the scenes and dramas throughout the novel, as does Ishmael tell Captain Ahab's story in *Moby Dick*. Huckleberry Finn in Twain's novel, and the Invisible Man in Ralph Ellison's 1952 novel of that title, however, are also the central characters, and they relate the details of their own fictional lives.

The use of second-person pronouns in narrative is less common, requiring the narrator to tell 'you' what to see and think throughout an entire narrative. Such narrators do often appear in epistolary novels or novels written in the form of letters exchanged among characters which readers observe either as a fly on the wall when the novels contain both sides of the correspondence or as a vicarious stand-in for the addressee when only one set of letters is narrated. In those cases, both the narrators and narratees (the 'you' being addressed) are characters within the story; they are what Genette calls intradiegetic, existing in the world of the narrative itself. Jamaica Kincaid's *A Small Place* (1988) begins with a shocking use of second-person pronouns as the narrator's voice tells 'you' what you will see when you visit the tiny island of Antigua. In this case, the narrator is what Genette (1980, pp. 244–5) calls heterodiegetic, meaning absent from the story, speaking from a different time, place, or even level of consciousness than the characters contained within the narrative. Surprisingly, though, Kincaid makes her readers ('you') hypothetically intradiegetic characters as it is those readers, the ones to whom the story is narrated, who would travel from the airport, feel the island's heat, check into a resort hotel, and walk along the beach.

Of course, just as with genre, texts may combine or shift among levels of narrative, points of view and voice in order to create different effects upon readers.

As Genette's concept of narrative level suggests, narrators telling the story in any person or voice may be more or less knowledgeable of their characters' interior lives. *Omniscient* narrators may know everything about the people and world in their narratives. They may reveal events of which the characters are unaware, or they may expose the characters' internal thoughts and desires – even those that run counter to their actions. The playful and experimental 2006 film *Stranger than Fiction* explores what happens to a character whose life is narrated by an omniscient narrator. The *protagonist* or main character, Harold Crick, awakes one morning to hear his every movement being described in the third-person by an omniscient narrator. When the narrator's voice announces, 'little did he know' his actions would lead to his death, Harold spends the rest of the film attempting to reclaim his own first-person narrative control over his life.

On the opposite end of the spectrum from Harold's external narrator, narratives told in *stream of consciousness* style embed their narrators (either in first-person or third-person) so deeply within a single character's thoughts that the narrator can be pulled erratically from the present moment to a deep memory or can be so distracted by the character's moods and associations that even a simple flower can trigger an intense flashback in time to the character's childhood or a moment of loss. The term 'stream of consciousness' was first applied to literature by May Sinclair in her 1918 review, 'The Novels of Dorothy Richardson'. As a narrative strategy, stream of consciousness developed out of the early twentieth-century growth in psychoanalysis and attention to the interplay between humans' conscious and unconscious desires. This twentieth-century literary innovation allowed writers to experiment with nonlinear, irrational, fragmented, and unchronological ways of telling stories. Furthermore, it opened up new possibilities for plots and conflicts. No longer did the conflict need to come from outside the character; instead, the character's own internal battles for meaning and purpose could make a simple walk down the street into a trial and tragedy of great proportions. As in Joyce's stream of consciousness story 'The Dead', Gabriel Conroy's thoughts and emotions turn a three-minute dance into an inquisition into his political loyalties. The path of his thoughts winds through the dance, back into his memories, his intellectual insecurities, his self-consciousness in his marriage, his plans for the future, and his struggle to establish a class status above the rest of his community. Externally, it may be just a dance, but internally, the scene is part of the tragedy of Gabriel's life.

As we see in the two examples above, some narrators are *extradiegetic*, disconnected from their characters, constrained as to what they can observe or quote, almost like a newspaper reporter, while others bridge that distance. *Limited omniscient* narrators may know everything about a single character, but view all other actions and events from the outside. By offering extra details and greater access to insights about a single character, such narratives are *internally focalized* upon a character (Genette 1992) and provide a biased filter that leads readers to sympathise with that character's views. In Nella Larsen's *Passing* (1929), for example, the third person narrator often attempts to remain distant from the characters, quoting letters and conversations without commentary, describing the settings and appearance of characters, and leaving many of readers' questions unanswered. However, the plot follows only Irene Redfield's actions, centres upon only her emotional state, reports only her conversations, and occasionally explains and even seems to enter Irene's excited thoughts.

The literary term for the narrative style in *Passing* that blurs the lines between the distant third-person narrator and the interior experience of a character is *free indirect discourse*, named for its free, unlabelled shifts from narrative description to quotation of a character's thoughts or speech. No quotation marks directly show the readers that the narrator is now in the character's head, but suddenly the narrator's sentences take on the voice, the speech patterns, even the emotional intensity of the focalized character. In *Passing*, the shift to free indirect discourse often happens subtly and gradually. As Irene reflects upon her meeting with an old acquaintance and her promise to visit the next Tuesday, the narrator informs us, 'She had, she told herself, no inclination to speak of a person who held so low an opinion of her loyalty, or her discretion. And certainly she had no desire or intention of making the slightest effort about Tuesday. Nor any other day for that matter' (Larsen 1929, p. 49). Although the passage begins by separating the narrator's words from what Irene 'told herself', by the end, Irene's indignation has so overtaken the narrator, that the sentences degrade into fragments clearly aligned with Irene's inner thoughts.

A text with free indirect discourse can seem realistic and even-handed, as if our narrator is giving an objective account, but a careful literary analysis reveals that we know only part of the story, part that may be muddied by the character's jealousies and fears. In the case of *Passing*, the narrator's limited perspective causes some uncertainty over what to believe about Irene when the text ends in a terrible accident, yet we remain confident in the narrator's ability to tell the story. In other cases, an *unreliable narrator* betrays so many flaws or biases that it is difficult to give the narrator much credibility at all. In 'How to make a close reading', we have already considered Nick Carraway's questionable judgement as the narrator of *The Great Gatsby*. The 2013 Bas Luhrmann film adaptation casts even further doubt on Nick's reliability by making him a patient in a mental hospital.

Thus far, most of my examples of narrative have come from films or *novels*, but narrative plot is also essential to long, *epic* poems involving a hero or, increasingly today, a heroine who undertakes an extensive quest, often lasting years or even decades and including obstacles and challenges that reflect the significant values and traditions of their place and time (e.g. Dante's *Divine Comedy* or Homer's *The Odyssey*). Although we refer to the voice of the poem as the 'speaker', such speakers can narrate their poems from any of the points of view outlined above. The speaker of a *dramatic monologue*, for instance, addresses his or her listeners as 'you' throughout the one-sided conversation that makes up the poem. Through the subtle use of the speaker's statements as a fictional persona, dramatic monologues evoke a whole scene as if we have flipped to a single page of a much longer conversation between that character and some others. Robert Browning's 'My Last Duchess' (1842), perhaps the best known dramatic monologue in English poetry, reveals the obsessive jealousy of the Duke as he comments to his visitor about a portrait of his first wife. The result is an alarming glimpse into her life and a foreshadowing of the dismal future of the woman he plans to marry next. The narrative snapshot in the poem contains a full plot conveyed through the first-person voice of the poem's speaker.

While narrative is the most important structure for content in any genre, *metre* is arguably the most significant device for organizing the form of literature. Outside of literary analysis, a metre is a unit for measuring length or distance, and in literature as well, the metre offers a means of measurement. In our case, the metre describes the length of the line of verse as measured by the number of syllables in the words. The type of metre also indicates the pattern of stressed and softer, unstressed syllables within the line. Perhaps the simplest way to understand metre is to recall that literature began as an oral art form, often performed with musical accompaniment. To help performers and audiences remember long, oral verse, poets used a regular rhythm or pattern of beats (stressed syllables) as well as rhymes. With the regular beats and rhyming words, listeners needed only to remember part of the poem, and the metrical structure (the pattern of the metre) would dictate the rest.

If a poem with regular rhyme and metre starts, 'If you were a cloud, I'd be your sky', the next line should have nine syllables and end with a long *i* sound: 'If you were a pear, I'd be your pie'. The rhythm of four louder, stressed syllables establishes a beat that limits the word choices. Here, the beat lands on the second syllable as in blues music, not on the first like the strong downbeat of a marching band. If we pursue the similarities between music and verse even further, the musical 'measure' makes a perfect analogy to the poetic *foot*. Written in common time, marches and ballads have four beats per measure; waltzes have three. Most poetic feet are shorter, either two or three syllables.

Iambic pentameter, the most common metre in English literature, refers to lines of five two-syllable feet (*penta*meter), alternating between an unstressed syllable and a stressed one. The pair of unstressed and stressed syllables become an *iamb*. Shakespeare's famous question – 'But soft, what light through yonder window breaks?' (1997, act 2, scene 2, line 2) – is a line of iambic pentameter in which 'soft', 'light', 'yon-', 'win-', and 'breaks' are naturally pronounced with greater stress than the other syllables and words. The stresses also emphasize the significant nouns and verbs in the sentence and downplay the less powerful parts of speech (conjunctions, adverbs, prepositions). In English, *blank verse* (unrhymed iambic pentameter) signifies formality, epic scale, the height of high literary culture. It appears throughout the centuries from John Milton's *Paradise Lost* (1667) to T. S. Eliot's *The Waste Land* (1922). English translators conventionally use blank verse to mark the formality of epic and classical world literature. Aristotle (1997, p. 8) states that the iambic rhythm most closely imitates natural speech, and the driving force of the metre can alter the structure of content and meaning of a text. Blank verse dominates Shakespeare's plays, but he often abandons it mid-play for prose or other poetic forms to demonstrate a shift in the character's status or state of mind.

The process of identifying the metre of poetry by counting syllables and marking stresses is called *scansion*. Although any of a variety of formal scansion systems can be applied, below is a basic rhythmic scan of our two simple lines:

Ĭf yóu | wĕre ă clóud, | Ĭ'd bé | yŏur ský.
Ĭf yóu | wĕre ă péar, | Ĭ'd bé | yŏur píe.

The cup-shaped symbol (*breve*) indicates an unstressed syllable, while the slash (acute accent) shows the stress. Vertical bars (the pipe symbol) show the separations between metrical feet. The majority of the lines have iambic feet. If these lines were part of a longer poem, they might continue to follow the iambic *tetrameter* (four feet per line) and four-line stanza (*quatrain*) pattern of a ballad. Within the lines, however, metrical variations disrupt the ballad rhythm. In both lines, the second foot requires us to rush through two unstressed syllables to reach our stressed syllable, creating a three-syllable foot with an *anapaestic* stress pattern, but since the extra syllable is unstressed (ă), it does not fundamentally upset the overall rhythm. In the third foot, there is so little difference in stress between 'I'd' and 'be' that the foot becomes a *spondee* (two stressed syllables), again without much overturning the pattern of the poem as a whole. Replace 'pear' with 'banana', how-ever, and the lines would change significantly:

Ĭf yóu wĕre | ă bă ná | nă, Ĭ'd bé | yŏur píe.

The result is *syncopation*, a rhythm in which attempting to follow the metre forces the stress to land on a normally unstressed syllable, such as 'were' in the first foot. Indeed, the choice of 'banana' disrupts the metre so much that we might call it *doggerel*, irregularity in rhythm due to poor technique or bad poetic choices. Despite these irregu-larities, scansion of a whole poem can reveal the underlying rhythmic pattern beating like a pulse beneath even unruly lines of verse.

Few poems follow any metre exactly, and those that do are often disparaged as tedious sing-song. Most poems written today, in fact, avoid regularity in metre and follow a *free verse* or *vers libre* style. Yet scansion can usefully identify the undercurrents that signal the metre and even the genre to which the poem belongs and thereby give clues to further meanings.

FIGURATIVE LANGUAGE AND TEXTUAL TACTICS

Beneath the large, structural layer, the detailed uses of *figurative language* generate aesthetic impressions at the sentence and line level. In contrast to literal language confined to the letter of the definition, figurative language extends the effects of words by defamiliarizing them and imbuing them with extra meaning. Lists of hundreds of literary and rhetorical figures can be found readily online. This section will define just a few. Words used as figures can function on multiple levels at once – as 'figures' like numbers representing complex, intangible concepts, as 'figures' in illustrations portraying concrete systems of interrelated parts, or as the 'figures' of the word's visual and aural shape which may recall similar words with very different meanings.

In this last sense, the material experience of the sight and sound of words carries additional content. Nowhere is this more apparent than in the use of *rhyme*. Recall the pleasure children take in rhymes as they experiment with the feel of words on their still-developing tongues. What do you call an enclosure full of flowers? A 'bloom room'. What is a shoplifter in a bookstore? A 'book crook'. *Perfect rhymes* like these foster predictability not only in the *end rhyme* of the final words of poetic lines, but in other literary forms as well. Hewey, Dewey, and Louie were Donald Duck's nephews in innumerable Disney cartoons. Even Salman Rushdie employed rhyme in his 1983 novel *Shame* to link the characters Chunni, Munnee, and Bunny in a preternatural bond of sisterhood.

Other rhymes can instill discord or dissonance in the text by promising a connection that never comes. A *slant rhyme* introduces a mismatch in the sounds of the final syllable of the rhymed words, as in 'tune'–'loom' or 'sixteen'–'kitchen'. Similarly, an *eye rhyme* appears to be a perfect rhyme, but falls short when pronounced (e.g. 'prove'–'love'). Not to be dismissed as mistakes, these partial rhymes use the surprising sensory experience of the words to alert readers to possible disconnections and interruptions in the content. If it behooves me to prove to you my love, the jarring eye rhyme might hint at a possible flaw in the quality of my emotion as well.

Figurative language can take advantage of the sensory qualities of words, but words can also be used to create sensory experiences through *imagery*. Including all senses, not just sight, vivid, descriptive imagery weaves an illusion of the sounds, smells, sights, feel, or taste of the objects being described. In Rita Dove's 'The Bistro Styx', the speaker, Demeter, meets her daughter Persephone in a Paris restaurant after she has been seduced by Hades. Demeter conveys the depths of her daughter's hunger through detailed imagery of the food she eats: the 'golden globe' of rich, ripe Camembert cheese, the 'dripping mess' of tear-drop slices of pear, and wine as dark as blood (Dove 1995, p. 42). The imagery carries readers beyond the menu into the sensual experience of the meal.

Through figurative language, words inspire readers to imagine both physical realities and abstract, intellectual concepts. Arguably the most important literary figures, *metaphors* ask readers to suspend limited, logical definitions to create new, intuitive definitions by comparison. A metaphor compares unrelated objects in order to convey a direct understanding of characteristics both share when literal explanations of those qualities would simply fail. In 'The Bistro Styx', for instance, the speaker attempts to describe the changes in her daughter's personality, which has become less forceful and vibrant since meeting Hades. But how do we define the intangible qualities of personal 'force' and 'vibrancy'? Rather than struggling with psychological terminology, the poem calls upon a metaphor: Persephone is a 'lipstick ghost on tissue' (Dove 1995, p. 41). The lipstick evokes sexual potency, beauty, health, and femininity, and its erasure onto the fragile paper demonstrates its diminishing power. Where the rational explanation sounds overly analytical and lacks the deep sense of loss and concern the mother feels in witnessing the change, the metaphor translates the entire force of the thought instantly into four, little words.

Like metaphors, *similes* also generate meaning through comparison, but they more clearly identify the two objects by using the words 'like' or 'as' to introduce the comparison. Dove's poem uses a simile to note that the Chateaubriand filet is 'like' a heart pulled out as a trophy of battle (Dove 1995, p. 42). The presence of 'like' guides readers to make deeper connections on a figurative level.

Simile and metaphor translate meaning across full comparisons, but *metonymy* and *synecdoche* create meaning by shifting the focus to a part of an object. In metonymy, an object's name is replaced by the name of an object associated with it; synecdoches substitute the name of a part of the object in place of the whole. The terms 'new money' and 'old money' are examples of metonymy for different segments of upper-class society. 'Old money' really refers to the families of long-standing reputation and generations of wealth and property-holdings, but the metonymy of the economic capital associated with them encourages readers to view particular qualities of the people being described. In Fitzgerald's *The Great Gatsby*, Daisy is often described through synecdoche as a voice. In climactic scenes, she does not act; instead, the voice pleads to leave, the voice is lost. Separating out her voice, which Gatsby already described as sounding like money, strips her of warmth and robs her of the ability to control her life. The synecdoche demonstrates this effect much more dramatically than a straightforward description of the plot events could do.

When metaphors or metonymies gain widespread recognition or recur throughout a text, they can assume the status of a *symbol*, an object used to represent a larger idea or concept. Symbols commonly appear in everyday life: the rose corresponds to love, the cross stands for Christian faith, the ring symbolizes marriage. Symbols both create a shorthand for referring to the larger concept and translate that concept into a tangible object that can relate metaphorically to other images and objects in the text. Many beginning readers approach literary analysis as a quest for symbols, but it is important to note that many powerful images are not symbols at all. While the green light at the end of Daisy's dock may indeed symbolize Gatsby's envy, the oranges in his orange juice maker are not symbols of autumn or harvest: they are just mixers for hundreds of party cocktails.

By building upon symbolic shorthand, writers can create complex, symbolic narratives about abstract concepts or *allegories*. An allegory relies upon symbols for places, characters, plot events, and other narrative elements in order to transform the surface story into a reflection of larger issues. From the title alone of *The Pilgrim's Progress from This World to That Which Is to Come*, John Bunyan makes his allegory quite overt. As his character Christian Pilgrim journeys from the City of Destruction to the Celestial City, he overcomes spiritual temptations in order to reach heaven (Bunyan 1678). Art Speigelman's graphic novel *Maus* (1997) directly narrates his father's story of surviving the Holocaust, but it uses a visual allegory by representing Jews as vulnerable mice, Nazis as predatory cats, and non-Jewish Poles as pigs, an unkosher animal. The X-Men comics offer a more complex allegory of the tragedy of discrimination in society. First published in 1963 by Stan Lee, the X-Men, members of a mutated race of humans, struggle to mask their differences from other humans in order to avoid persecution. In their civil rights era context, these mutations can allegorize racial difference, but Magneto, the main mutant villain, also launches a campaign of mutant superiority over humans and strives variously to rule, transform, or eliminate humanity in an allegory of Nazi genocide (Lee and Kirby 2002). In later decades, the series added further twists to these allegorical interpretations by making Magneto himself a Jewish Holocaust survivor who will go to any lengths to protect mutants from a similar fate (Pak and DiGiandomenico 2009).

Through these and dozens of literary figures and structures, literature embeds multiple meanings within single narratives, sentences, and lines. The aim is to convey the richness of experience – its ambivalences, contradictions, complexities – through aesthetic interactions with readers. The tools of close reading unravel these interwoven layers of meaning and reveal the wealth of language in the texts we read.

REFERENCES AND FURTHER READING

Abrahms, M. H. and Harpham, G. G. (2014) *A Glossary of Literary Terms*, 11th ed., Stamford, CT: Cengage Learning.

Aristotle (1997) *Poetics*, trans. M. Heath, New York: Penguin.

Barthes, R. (1975) 'An Introduction to the Structural Analysis of Narrative', trans. L. Duisit, *New Literary History*, vol. 6, no. 2, pp. 237–272.

Brooks, C. (1975) *The Well Wrought Urn*, San Diego, CA: Harcourt, Brace.

Brower, R. (1951) *The Fields of Light: An Experiment in Critical Reading*, Oxford: Oxford University Press.

Bunyan, J. (1678) *The Pilgrim's Progress from This World to That Which Is to Come*, London: Haddon.

Derrida J. (1980) 'The Law of Genre', trans. A Ronnell, *Glyph*, vol. 7, pp. 202–232.

Dove, R. (1995) *Mother Love*, New York: W.W. Norton.

Dubrow, H. (1982) *Genre*, London: Methuen.

Duff, D. (ed.) (2000) *Modern Genre Theory*, London and New York: Longman, Pearson Education.

Erlich, V. (1980) *Russian Formalism: History-Doctrine*, 4th ed., trans. W. de Gruyter, The Hague: Mouton Publishers.

Fitzgerald, F. S. (1925) *The Great Gatsby*, New York: Charles Scribner's Sons.

Forché, C. (1981) *The Country Between Us*, New York: HarperCollins.

Frow, J. (2006) *Genre: The New Critical Idiom*, London and New York: Routledge.

Gallop, J. (2010) 'Close Reading in 2009', *ADE Bulletin*, vol. 149, pp. 15–19.

Genette, G. (1980) *Narrative Discourse: An Essay in Method*, trans. J. E. Lewin, Ithaca, NY: Cornell University Press.

Genette, G. (1992) *The Architext: An Introduction*, trans. J. E. Lewin, Berkeley: University of California Press.

Green, D. (2003) 'Literature Itself: The New Criticism and Aesthetic Experience', *Philosophy and Literature*, vol. 27, no. 2, pp. 62–79.

Greene, R. (2012) *The Princeton Encyclopedia of Poetry and Poetics*, 4th ed., Princeton, NJ: Princeton University Press.

Guillory, J. (2008) 'On the Presumption of Knowing How to Read', *ADE Bulletin*, vol. 145, pp. 8–11.

Hall, D. (1993) *The Unsayable Said: An Essay*, Port Townsend, Washington: Copper Canyon.

Joyce, J. (1914) *Dubliners*, London: Grant Richards.

Larsen, N. (1929) *Passing*, New York: Knopf.

Lee, S. and Kirby, J. (2002) *Marvel Masterworks: The X-Men vol. 1*, New York: Marvel Comics Group.

Moretti, F. (2013) *Distant Reading*, London: Verso.

Pak, G. and DiGiandomenico, C. (2009) *X-Men: Magneto Testament*, New York: Marvel.

Plato (1992) *The Republic*, trans. G. M. A. Grube, Indianapolis and Cambridge: Hackett.

Richards, I. A. (1930) *Practical Criticism: A Study of Literary Judgment*, London: Kegan Paul, Trench, Trubner and Co.

Robinson, K. (2008) *Changing Paradigms*, [Video file], Royal Society for the Encouragement of Arts, Manufactures and Commerce, London, Available from: http://www.thersa.org/events/video/archive/sir-ken-robinson [Accessed 12th November 2012].

Rushdie, S. (1983) *Shame*, New York: Knopf.

Shakespeare, W. (1997) *The Tragedy of Romeo and Juliet*, in G. B. Evans and J. J. M. Tobin (eds.), *The Riverside Shakespeare*, Boston: Houghton Mifflin.

Shklovsky, V. (1965) 'Art as Technique', in L. T. Lemon and M. J. Reiss (eds.) *Russian Formalist Criticism: Four Essays*, Lincoln: University of Nebraska Press.

Sinclair, M. (1918) 'The Novels of Dorothy Richardson', *The Egoist*, vol. 5, no. 4, pp. 57–59.

Spiegelman, A. (1997) *The Complete Maus*, New York: Pantheon.

Stranger than Fiction. (2006) Film. Directed by Marc Forster. [DVD] USA: Columbia Pictures.

Todorov, T. (1976) 'The Origin of Genres', trans. R. M. Berrong, *New Literary History*, vol. 8, no. 1, pp. 159–170.

Twain, M. (1885) *Adventures of Huckleberry Finn: Tom Sawyer's Comrade*, New York: Charles Webster and Co.

Warner, M. (2004) 'Uncritical Reading,' in Gallop, J. (ed.) *Polemic: Critical or Uncritical*, New York and London, Routledge.

Wellek, R. and Warren, A. (1984) *Theory of Literature*, San Diego, CA: Harcourt, Brace.

ANALYSIS IN CONTEXT

The last chapter, 'Close reading: words and forms', focused nearly exclusively on the words on the page. This chapter moves one step outward as it examines the relationship between the **text** and its time and place of publication. It summarises the significant cultural and historical factors that relate to **literary** production and contribute to meaning.

Based on the principles of New Criticism and Practical Criticism, readers often believe that 'great literature' and literary **classic**s are 'timeless'. We say masterpieces transcend the particulars of their own time and place to offer universal messages to readers throughout the centuries. In many ways, this is true, and **close reading** alone can help us uncover those truths. If our goal is literary analysis, however, we cannot be satisfied with broad universal messages. We must pursue truth and meaning down deeper avenues for interpretation as well. A major limitation of close reading lies in its emphasis on the transcendent artistry of form over the particulars of social and historical references. In his study of literary theory, critic Terry Eagleton asserts that practitioners of New Criticism and Practical Criticism wanted literature to be 'plucked free of the wreckage of history and hoisted into a sublime space above it' (1996, p. 42). Seeking an escape from the complicated problems of their war-torn time, they promoted a definition of literature as art that could rise above difficult, everyday existence and neglected to address the many ways literature actually represents and comments upon the details of that difficult, everyday life. As a result, close reading excels at explaining how texts are written but cannot always answer why they are written that way. On its own, the New Critical methodology does not effectively reveal the social work texts perform by participating in or even sparking political and cultural debates.

If we want to reach a fuller analysis of literature, then context matters. It matters whether or not Toni Morrison's *A Mercy* (2008) is an eighteenth-century text or a twenty-first-century one about eighteenth-century slavery. It matters whether Kurt Vonnegut's *Slaughterhouse-Five, or the Children's Crusade: A Duty-Dance with Death* (1969) was written in the middle of the World War II bombing of Dresden which it describes or in the middle of the Vietnam War wreaking havoc on a new generation of soldiers and civilians. Is it subversive for Fanny Price in Jane Austen's *Mansfield Park* (1814) to enquire about the slave trade when her uncle returns from business in Antigua, or is it quite acceptable at the time? Contextual analysis attempts to answer such questions.

As a concept, **context** is not difficult to understand. When we remind our friends not to take our words 'out of context', we ask them to consider the way meaning is shaped by the circumstances surrounding our speech. An array of culture, news, manners, trends, and even language patterns abound inside, outside and around every text, creating shared understandings of references to events and social values that establish a context both for authors and readers. Thus, while the idea of context is rather simple, its application in literary analysis must take into account a wide range of factors.

In our *Mansfield Park* example, the text notes that Fanny asks her uncle a question about the slave trade. He answers, but his daughters do not join in the conversation, and, feeling self-conscious about her interest, Fanny drops that line of discussion. On a purely textual level, the words of the scene emphasize the difference between Fanny (the niece) and her cousins (the daughters), but when we consider the context, several other meanings come to the fore.

If we read without attention to the date of the publication, much of the novel seems rather petty; its conflicts arise primarily from the family's different responsibilities to its children based on gender and birth order. But when we use the publication date to guide our interpretation, seemingly minor details start to signify complex social critiques. For instance, in 1814, women like Fanny would have no opportunities for pursuing business careers; therefore, her curiosity about her uncle's work sets her apart from typical members of her gender. As an early nineteenth-century female character, Fanny exhibits an unusual intellectual ability and awareness of public concerns. This contextual detail implies that Fanny's self-consciousness stems not only from her difference in familial status, but from her challenge to gender norms of the time.

In 1814, Fanny's creator, author Jane Austen, also stood out as an unusually successful woman writer. Although women writers were becoming increasingly common and, in fact, grew in popularity throughout the nineteenth-century, they were often confined to less prestigious **genre**s and seen as unartistic, 'low-brow', or even indecent – not elite writers. Austen achieved greater recognition than most of her female peers, but this problem of status served as an important context for her novel and its audience as well. Indeed, Austen's name does not appear on the title page of *Mansfield Park*, though the publisher notes the book is by the author of *Sense and Sensibility* and *Pride and Prejudice*.

Extending the context in ever wider circles, we notice that Britain was embroiled in a range of wars from the beginning of the nineteenth century, including wars against France, Russia, and the USA. The text notes Fanny's own father is a disabled lieutenant in the marines, her brother joins the navy, and society is always in need of soldiers, though military professions rarely offer paths to economic prosperity. Instead, the text holds up the colonies – in the Caribbean and the 'East' – as sites where fortunes could be made. Fanny's uncle stays in Antigua for two years in order to protect his own wealth, and it is in the context of his return that Fanny brings up the slave trade. The novel reveals no details of her question or her uncle's answer. Readers must draw on the context to interpret the meaning of the passage. Significantly, the slave trade was outlawed throughout the British Empire in 1807 (though slavery itself remained legal when the novel was published). Certainly the characters would avoid 'impolite' questions about a black market for illegal slave trading or the slaves' response to the law, but Fanny could ask her uncle more generally about the effects of the end of the slave trade. If so, a literary analysis based on context would attempt to determine how that implied question fits with her other comments about sincerity, service to others, and morality. Through the combination of close reading and contextual analysis, we can draw conclusions about the text's position on both the status of women and the slavery debate.

HISTORY AND LITERATURE, LITERATURE AS HISTORY

With *Mansfield Park*, Austen gives readers a window into the experiences and concerns of the past. At the same time, the details presented may change the way readers feel about those concerns and may pave the way for a culture more open to social mobility and opportunities for women. In literary studies, the theory of New Historicism explains this interdependence of history and literature. A major tenet of New Historicism is that literature is inseparable from other modes of culture. In contrast to New Criticism and Practical Criticism, New Historicism believes that literature both is shaped by history and shapes it.

Following that logic, literary analysis not only can uncover the aesthetic dimensions of texts, but can also help us understand the cultures in which literature was produced and which literature itself influenced. Adding some New Historicist methods to our literary analysis toolkit can expand our interpretations of literature and enhance our close readings of texts.

Consider the way the post-9/11 cultural climate has shaped literature, and the way that literature has shaped our cultural views of privacy, surveillance, law enforcement and security. The BBC series *Spooks* (or *MI-5*), which ran from 2002-2011, dramatised the violence and danger in the lives of intelligence officers and explored the traumas and moral dilemmas they face in attempting to prevent a variety of terrorist threats. The show both fed upon global anxieties about terrorism and heightened the audience's collective sense that such attacks were always looming just beyond the reach of our surveillance networks.

Similarly, *The Cosby Show*, which aired on NBC television from 1984 to 1992, featuring Bill Cosby as Cliff Huxtable, an upper-middle class African American doctor married to an African American lawyer. Their family lives in New York City where the children succeed in school, with the eldest a college graduate. History shaped the show which reflected the post–Civil Rights era growth in numbers of affluent, professional African Americans in a booming mid-1980s economy. In turn, *The Cosby Show* shaped history by becoming the first top-rated show in the USA to feature a predominantly African American cast. Holding its number one ranking for five consecutive seasons, *The Cosby Show* broadcast images of successful African Americans into millions of living rooms worldwide and countered stereotypes about African American families and careers.

In recent years, other contextual events have recast the show in a new light. Widely-reported accusations against Bill Cosby have embroiled him, and consequently his legacy as a performer, in a scandal of harassment of women and sexual assault. In this new context, today's audiences approach Cosby's fictional characters through the lens of their criticism and scepticism about him. Sullied by the scandal, Cosby's fictional characters seem less sympathetic and wholesome, and television networks have pulled reruns of *The Cosby Show* and cancelled plans to create a new Cosby-based television series. In this case, the influence of history and culture upon audiences has called new attention to gender representations within the show and reshaped the meaning of the text decades after it was produced.

To analyse texts in their context, then, is to analyse our cultures, our histories, and ourselves along with our written forms of art. A text's historical and cultural context helps to define the most popular content, conflicts, and issues trending in literature; the types of readers and audiences available to enjoy it; the institutional support and training afforded to writers; and the openness to innovation or rootedness in tradition in the culture of the time. Recognizing these contextual factors, we acknowledge that authors may write privately and personally, but texts require public backing and approval in order to reach audiences. In their public forms, texts may be the victims or darlings of history, and they may intervene in that history with words that change the world.

For example, today we read Niccolò Machiavelli's *The Prince* (1998) as a stunning example of political philosophy. His advice to leaders that the ends justify the means still can shock our sense of justice, yet the beauty and power of his language entice modern audiences as much as they did his own contemporaries. How can awareness of historical context help us analyse and interpret *The Prince*?

Given the choice, Machiavelli did not prefer a political system ruled by princes, monarchs, and autocrats. He was part of Florence's republican government before the Medici family seized control of the city in 1512. The city's new governor, Giuliano de'Medici, arrested and tortured Machiavelli in 1513, but soon cleared him of charges of conspiracy. Machiavelli's torture and loss of status shape the text – whether consciously or not.

Within months, Machiavelli wrote *The Prince* and attempted to convince the Medici family to become his political patrons and welcome him back to the leadership of Florence. The book's context lies in this moment of political turmoil for the city and personal crisis for the author. Again, history matters. Italian Renaissance writers and artists did not gain wealth by selling their work; they relied upon commissions and favours from patrons among the nobility or the church. Machiavelli's political future and economic prosperity – not to mention safety from further torture – depended on the Medici family's appreciation of the manuscript, but they did not respond. Instead, the manuscript was shared privately under the title *About Principalities*, and *The Prince* did not see formal publication until 1532, five years after Machiavelli's death and over a decade after the death of Lorenzo de'Medici of Florence, to whom the book is dedicated.

Although we may read *The Prince* as if it enjoys the kind of absolute power it describes, during its time, it was a minor, unpublished treatise by a controversial, out-of-favour writer. For a brief period in the decades after it was published, its relevance to Italian and European political problems and its bold claims lifted it to prominence, but by 1559, Pope Paul IV placed all of Machiavelli's writings on the *Index of Prohibited Books*. According to the nineteenth-century scholar of Elizabethan drama, Edward Meyer (1897, p. 1), British Renaissance playwrights and other writers represented Machiavelli as 'the very devil incarnate, or, at least, as the incorporation of all hypocrisy'. There were even rumours that Machiavelli's *Prince* inspired King Henry VIII to break from the Catholic Church and establish the Church of England. For nearly one hundred years, *The Prince* was on the losing side of history. Its meaning, then, derives not from a privileged consideration of the ideal political system, but in reaction to particular political realities it hoped (and failed) to change.

History can affect the way books are produced, released, and received by audiences. It can also place severe limits upon the content. In colonial American literature of the 1600s, sermons, religious poetry, histories, travel writing, and captivity narratives dominate the literary scene, as if the writers in the early colonies were bound by the realities of their landscape, their interactions with Native Americans, and their desire for divine purpose, redemption, and aid. Historical context can help explain the narrow scope of this content.

Colonial America had few publishing venues and even fewer educational institutions. Those were centred in the early cities of Boston and Philadelphia and mainly dedicated to publishing church and government documents, training ministers, and converting Native Americans to Christianity. Religious literature, therefore, had an advantage over other forms in reaching early American readers. Much other writing by colonial Americans was published in England for British audiences interested in reports of exotic adventure in the New World. The captivity narrative genre offered a profitable combination of the other literary strains. The stories blended the shock of capture by Native Americans with the adventure of witnessing native cultures while held hostage in their homes, the religious inspiration of maintaining faith in adversity, and, usually, the joy of redemption when rescue returned the captive to her devout Christian community. In the early American context, the history of presses, literary markets, transportation, political and religious policies, and economic pressures shaped the literature as much as or more than the talents of individual writers.

When we consider the relationship between literature and history, the economy, politics, religion, science, psychology, art, linguistics, and culture all play roles in shaping literary meaning. Attempting to read without an awareness of historical context can produce misinterpretations of the text, yet most readers interested in literary analysis can benefit from understanding just two main historical contexts: literary history and cultural history. Basic literary history describes the shifts and changes in literary methods, genres, authors, and forms. Cultural history examines the social customs, values, and societal divisions of the past. Those two histories will be the focus of the sections that follow.

LITERARY PERIODS AND MOVEMENTS: COMMUNITIES OF WRITERS

Immersing themselves in contextual background, scholars of New Historicism specialize in particular time periods so narrowly that they gain a complex picture of life for their featured writers – from fashion to faith, from medicine to marriage. Such intimate knowledge, however, is not necessary for contextually-informed literary analysis. In general, relating literary texts to the broad themes and concerns of their context in blocks of centuries or generations can highlight characteristic concerns that open up new meanings and interpretations. In literary studies, we refer to these divisions as *literary periods*.

Conventional literary periods are used to categorize literature in terms of both genre and content. By situating texts within their literary periods, we gain greater appreciation of their level of artistic innovation, influence, and even revolution. According to Professor Ted Underwood (2013, p. 2), author of *Why Literary Periods Mattered*, 'the value of literary study, in the eyes of students and of society at large, has been durably bound up with its ability to define cultural moments and contrast them against each other' and against the present time. Literary periods offer a snapshot of history's shifts and changes and help to crystallize the characteristics of different eras. Where historians seek to know what happened in particular periods, literary scholars want to grasp their life experience and understand the ways in which language and literary genres encapsulated that experience for the time.

Woody Allen's 2011 film *Midnight in Paris* humorously depicts the attachment of readers to past literary periods. The main character, a writer filled with nostalgia for literary modernism, magically travels back in time to the bars and salons of 1920s Paris where he talks with Ernest Hemingway, Gertrude Stein, F. Scott Fitzgerald, and a dozen other literary and artistic idols. The film illustrates the danger of oversimplifying literary periods and attempting to make their 'cultural moments' too blissfully distinct. Literary critics also raise questions about the validity of dividing literature, or history itself, into periods when so many changes unfold gradually and when our own cultural perspectives and interests colour our views of what makes a period significant. Some have disparaged literary

ANCIENT & CLASSICAL	Medieval	Renaissance	Enlightenment	Romanticism	VICTORIAN		Postcolonial & Global	
3000BCE-450CE	450-1485	1485-1660	1660-1790	1798-1832	1837-1901		1901-Present	
			1660-1680		1830-1865	1850-1930	1810-1850	1950-Present
			RESTORATION		American Renaissance	Realism	Modernism	Postmodern & Contemporary

Figure 3.1 Timeline of literary history with overlapping periods

periods for following a 'Eurochronology' and proposed radically different approaches based on a 'world-oriented history of modern literature' (Hayot 2012, pp. 6, 8). Today's scholars debate *periodization* (the study of dividing literature into periods) as much as they do the **literary canon** (Besserman 1996), and the overlapping boundaries, fluctuating dates, and name changes of literary periods attest to the complexity of historical study and the impossibility of identifying the exact moment a cultural paradigm changes (see Figure 3.1).

Nonetheless, classification of literary periods usefully highlights commonalities based on the intellectual, spiritual, moral, religious, and political questions preoccupying different generations. Periodization also calls attention to the media and technology used to produce and distribute literature in a particular time (e.g. **oral literature** v. print). The dominance and emergence of different genres; poetic, dramatic, and **narrative** structures; preferred types of characters and narrators; and even typical subject matter all serve to group literature into historical periods. Using digital techniques of linguistic analysis, scholars have recently expanded our understanding of the common range of vocabulary, sentence length, use of punctuation, amount of dialogue, and other linguistic features shared by texts produced within the same literary period. With literary periods serving as a baseline for contextual analysis of literature, we improve our understanding of the expectations the original audiences would have brought to a text and the extent to which the text met or challenged them.

TIMELINE OF LITERARY PERIODS

The overview of literary periods in this section outlines the characteristics and classic texts of the broad divisions common in English and American literary studies while also drawing connections to world literature. It is important to note, however, that many periods can be broken into sub-categories, and both names and dates of periods vary based on the nationality of the literature being studied.

ANCIENT PERIOD 4000 BCE–800 BCE

Throughout this enormous span of time, technological limitations of transportation and publication kept literature focused on local audiences, though the content often aimed to answer lofty questions about the nature of humanity and the divine, as in the *Vedas* of Indian literature, the Egyptian *Book of the Dead*, the *Epic of Gilgamesh*, oral Hebrew literature, and, at the end of the period, Homer's *The Iliad* and *The Odyssey*.

Ancient literature was mostly oral, based in live performances, often accompanied by music and/or dance, narrated by storytellers who were not identified as authors since the purpose of the literature was seen as communal and its source often divine inspiration. Even Homer credits the muses for singing or telling him the stories in his epic poems. In fact, conflicting historical evidence cannot confirm the existence of a single man named Homer who produced these poems. The name Homer is an invention, applied centuries later to poetry attributed to one or more oral poets of the Homeridae guild once the poems were translated into written form.

The written literature of the ancient period was produced in expensive media – clay or stone tablets, leather parchment, and papyrus – by the few scribes literate in hierogylphics, cuneiform, ideograms, and other mostly pictorial linguistic systems. Though large empires and cities did periodically arise, little effort was made to cultivate international audiences, and most literary content aimed to convey religious beliefs, cultural customs, traditions, values, and histories within a single culture or region.

CLASSICAL PERIOD 800 BCE–450 CE

The refinement and standardization of various phonetic and alphabetic writing systems through expanding empires in the Mediterranean and Asia contributed to a growth in literature during the classical period, though many of the ancient themes continued throughout this time. Oral literature remained important, and drama rose in popularity through playwrights such as Sophocles and Euripides in Greece and Kalidasa in India. Philosophical, scientific, and historical texts by Plato, Socrates, and Aristotle; Confucian and Taoist writing in China; the Sanskrit *Upanishads* including the *Bhagavad Gita*; and the Christian bible were all produced on the wave of growing prosperity, increasing educational opportunities, and expanding communication networks. Aristotle's *Poetics* even attempted to codify the forms and rules of literature, defining it as a significant branch of both knowledge production and art. By the end of the classical period, Latin had become a global tongue, enabling translation and exchange of literature across several continents.

MEDIEVAL PERIOD 450–1485

While the Western stereotype of Medieval Europe remains a high-walled castle with a heavy drawbridge, in many ways the prevailing experience of this period was one of movement and encounter. The growth and spread of Islam, the global exchanges spawned by the Crusades, and international conquests among people in Europe, Asia, Africa, and South America also led to cross-cultural exchanges of stories, metaphors, and language. Recalling the unnamed Middle English poet of *Pearl* and *Gawain*, the owners of most of those castles spent the majority of their lives far outside their walls. This outward-looking perspective can be found in the Anglo-Saxon epic *Beowulf*, chivalric romances, tales of pilgrimage, such as Geoffrey Chaucer's *The Canterbury Tales*, Boccacio's *The Decameron*, and the travel literature of China's Song Dynasty.

At the same time that travel allowed readers and writers to pass beyond their local borders, a recognition of the value of local languages also spawned a reaction against Latin, Sanskrit, and other dominant literary languages. Vernacular poetry by Dante and Petrarch in Italian, Tamil poets in India, and Lou Guan Zhong in China all point to a growth in linguistic diversity. During this period, the invention of Chinese wood-block printing and the Gutenberg press with movable type as well as linen and textile-based paper reduced the costs of making multiple copies of literature and helped to usher in the explosion of publications in the centuries to come.

RENAISSANCE 1485–1660

Many scholars who study the Renaissance today prefer the title Early Modern to signal the transition to modern forms of language and culture during this period. In English, this means the abandonment of many of the Germanic endings on words and a growing influence of Romance languages in grammar and vocabulary. Literary scholars interested in historical context also use the term to emphasize:

- the end of feudalism in Europe;
- the emergence of a strong, merchant middle class worldwide;
- the contact between eastern and western hemispheres that gave us a modern map of the world;
- the outbreak of the Protestant Reformation that divided the power of the Catholic church;
- and the development of increasingly complex political structures that led to the consolidation of modern nations.

With the use of mechanical printing, the modern concept of authorship arose (though modern ideas of copyright and plagiarism did not). For the first time in literary history, most texts were published with the author's name printed on the title page.

The more common view of the Renaissance, however, remains valuable to understanding literature of the time. A renaissance or rebirth of attention to learning, art, science, and the values of the classical period drove tremendous productivity and innovation in literature. During this period William Shakespeare, Edmund Spenser, Christopher Marlowe, and John Milton wrote much of the literature that remains the foundation of the English literary canon today. Renaissance and Elizabethan English poetry no longer fought for status against texts written in Latin; they mastered the iambic pentameter form of blank verse in both poetry and drama and adapted the sonnet form from France and Italy to create the English love sonnet tradition. Poets like Sir Philip Sidney further formulated the secular purpose of fictional and imaginative literature by touting poetry's ability to use beauty and philosophy to inspire readers to virtue. Neither Sidney nor the other Elizabethan writers limited themselves to virtuous plots and characters, however, and their texts all display literary intricacy, moral ambivalence, and psychological complexity.

A similar embrace of literature and the arts occurred worldwide. India's Taj Mahal was built by the Mughal Empire, which also promoted Persian, Hindi, and Urdu literature. Contact with the Americas allowed for the publication of texts by and about indigenous American peoples in Spanish, English, Italian, and French. China's Ming Dynasty produced novels, including *Journey to the West*. The French *romans* also transitioned from poetry to prose, and Miguel de Cervantes produced the novel *Don Quixote* (1605–1615) in Spanish, marking a significant addition to the genres available for literary innovation.

ENLIGHTENMENT 1660–1790

Named for its emphasis on rationality, science, and education, the Enlightenment expanded the Renaissance interest in knowledge into different, increasingly prose-based, literary genres. Satire and comedy, including the Restoration Comedy plays of the first part of the period, brought a new edge of attack to literature. During the Restoration period in England (1660–1689), the return of the monarchy also relaxed the artistic regulations put in place under the religiously conservative commonwealth government. Literature responded with sexually-charged, witty plays and poems about the manners and amorality of the upper-class. Throughout the Enlightenment period and the bulk of the eighteenth century, satires like those of Alexander Pope, Jonathan Swift, and Voltaire continued to expose the hypocrisy of society and its institutions while nonfiction prose essays, letters, diaries, histories, biographies, and autobiographies by John Locke, Benjamin Franklin, Thomas Paine, Immanuel Kant, Thomas Jefferson, Mary Wollstonecraft, and Samuel Johnson attempted to define the rights of citizens, the responsibilities of governments, the nature of morality, and the social structures necessary to preserve human dignity and progress.

The prose novel also appeared in English published by British writers like Aphra Behn, Daniel Defoe, Henry Fielding, and Samuel Richardson, as well as by growing numbers of English-speaking Africans affected by the slave trade, such as Olaudah Equiano.

ROMANTICISM 1798–1832

The Romantic period in England is bookended by two, very specific literary events: William Wordsworth and Samuel Taylor Coleridge's 1798 publication of the *Lyrical Ballads* which celebrated the poet's imagination, emotion, and creative power, and the death in 1832 of Sir Walter Scott, a major novelist of the movement. In this view, Romanticism is driven by personality: it is born with the individual genius of its writers and dies when they do. The myriad poetic responses to the deaths of Romantic poets John Keats and Lord Byron further support this claim.

Viewed more broadly, however, the period is far more expansive. On a political timeline, Romanticism begins with the start of the French Revolution in 1789 and ends with the passage of the 1832 Reform Act which extended the vote to greater numbers of middle class citizens in England and Wales and partially institutionalized the Romantic spirit of reform. Romantic literature, then, serves as the voice of the exuberant exercise of human rights and the glorification of individual liberty against oppression as portrayed in William Blake's *Songs of Innocence and of Experience* (1789) and Percy Bysshe Shelley's *Prometheus Unbound* (1820).

Looking at Romanticism across national boundaries, the period begins in 1774 with Johann Wolfgang von Goethe's *The Sorrows of Young Werther* and ends with Transcendentalism (1830–1850) and the American Renaissance (1850–1865), whose writers include Ralph Waldo Emerson, Henry David Thoreau, and Walt Whitman. This international view also highlights the spectrum of the movement from its ecstatic, spiritual communion with the creative force of nature in poems like Whitman's *Leaves of Grass* (1855) to its dark and tortured, gothic consideration of the line between the natural and the supernatural in texts like Mary Shelley's *Frankenstein* (1818), Nathaniel Hawthorne's *House of the Seven Gables* (1851), and Edgar Allan Poe's 'The Fall of the House of Usher' (1839). Whether short or long, the Romanticist period paid tribute to the human capacity to transcend life's mundane obligations, to aspire to a higher, more spiritual awareness through an unfettered emotional and intellectual life, and to express that creative power through poetry and sometimes prose.

VICTORIAN PERIOD *1837–1901*

As with Romanticism, the Victorian period derives from British history, but the period shares significant overlaps with the more global period of Realism (1850–1930) and with American naturalism (1890–1915). Disillusioned or disappointed by the failure of Romanticism to achieve social change, Victorian literature, realism, and naturalism in different ways embodied a world in which everyday people struggle to maintain a sense of spiritual energy and virtue against the pressures of survival. Writers of realism sought to report those experiences clearly and objectively, without the unrestrained emotions that characterized Romanticism. The many realist novels produced during the period shared the empirical perspective of the scientific and political experiments driving change in industry and society.

For some of the more satirical writers near the end of the period, like Oscar Wilde and Mark Twain, humour was possible, but for most other writers of both poetry and prose (Emily and Charlotte Brontë, Charles Dickens, Gustave Flaubert, Alfred Tennyson, Thomas Hardy, Leo Tolstoy, Theodore Dreiser, Dante and Christina Rosetti, and Edith Wharton), the beauty of literature and life lay in the exercise of virtue despite the constant threat of poverty and the inescapable presence of death. The tragic grace of Hardy's title character in *Tess of the d'Urbervilles* (1892) who is seduced, disgraced, deceived, and ultimately collapses on the ancient rocks of Stonehenge offers an example of both the enduring purity and virtue within the character and the crushing realities that trap her in a life of sin and crime. In both English and world literature, the nineteenth century was filled with

- sentimental novels about foundlings and orphans whose moral goodness might help them find an appropriate home;
- sensational fiction about crimes, cons, adultery, and prostitution;
- slave narratives about the quest for freedom and the sacrifices necessary to escape the inhumanity and immorality of slavery;
- and long, social novels about the matches and marriage arrangements necessary to keep family fortunes and names intact.

By the end of the period, steam engines on rails and ships transported literature around the world in magazines and mass market novels printed on inexpensive, wood pulp paper. Political experiments with universal public education increased **literacy** rates and expanded markets for popular literature that stood in marked contrast to the carefully illustrated, craft printings of beautiful editions by Blake and other Romanticists. The nineteenth century's more realist and practical texts demonstrated the impact of the industrial revolution on both literary content and the physical book itself.

MODERNISM 1910–1950

The icon of modernism, the 1920s flapper dancing in a jazz club, conveys an image of freedom from the social constraints, tight collars, long skirts, dark colors, heavy hats, and oppressive etiquette of the Victorian and Edwardian periods. The deep connections between white modernists and African American writers of the Harlem Renaissance and New Negro Movement in the 1920s–1930s (e. g. W. E. B. Du Bois, Claude McKay, Zora Neale Hurston, and Langston Hughes) further signalled the period's interest in destroying tradition and shaking up society. Modernists like Ernest Hemingway, Muriel Rukeyser, W. H. Auden, George Orwell, Sylvia Townshend Warner, and Federico Garcia Lorca all wrote from and about Spain and its failed resistance to fascist takeover during the Spanish Civil War. Freedom and experimentation were modernism's stock in trade, but that freedom occurred in the midst of the violence, starvation, alienation, disorientation, and upheaval of two world wars and a global economic depression. Modernism thrived in these extremes.

While the nineteenth century focused externally on the structure and order of society, the twentieth century turned its gaze inward. As the monarchies, empires, and nations of the past crumbled, modernists sought authority and truth within themselves. Drawing upon the new field of psychoanalysis, modernists explored the limits of human knowledge and observation. If what we see is coloured by our unconscious desires, our moods, our memories, then we cannot trust that others will understand our observations in the same way that we do. Therefore, modernists abandoned the realist principle of conveying objective meaning and focused instead on creating innovative literary experiences for readers that would allow them to derive their own meanings in the act of reading.

The modernist period is known for its fragmented, free verse poetry – from Gertrude Stein's avant garde, ungrammatical poems about common objects to e. e. cummings's concrete poetry with the letters and words curving around the page in a text-based picture of their content. Reclaiming literature from Victorian and Edwardian mass audiences, modernist poets and other writers revived limited print editions with modernist art illustrations and stylistic innovation in the fonts and type. Modernists launched well-crafted magazines with small circles of subscribers. They formed tight literary circles and sponsored their own publications and prizes, supporting each other with reviews.

On the other hand, the modernists also embraced popular forms like film, radio, and the lecture circuit, and they cultivated public personas in magazines like *Vanity Fair, Cosmopolitan, Ladies' Home Journal, The Saturday Evening Post*, and *Life*. Poets T. S. Eliot, Ezra Pound, H.D. (Hilda Doolittle), Marianne Moore, and Gertrude Stein all conducted readings on the radio, reaching audiences who were introduced to modern poets through school and university classrooms throughout the 1940s. The BBC's Radio Programme Catalogue of the period reads like a Who's Who of modernist literature. Modern playwrights like Eugene O'Neill, Tennessee Williams, and Thornton Wilder, who produced some of the most exciting and experimental drama since the Elizabethan age, often sold the rights to their plays to film companies or worked on screenplays between stage projects. Fiction writers like William Faulkner and F. Scott Fitzgerald wrote for Hollywood too. For the first time, film and radio texts, like Fritz Lang's *Metropolis* (1927), Sergei Eisenstein's *Battleship Potemkin* (1925), *The Jazz Singer* (1927) starring Al Jolson, and Orson Welles's radio broadcast of *War of the Worlds* (1938), also entered the scope of literary modernism. Even Walt Disney's *Snow White and the Seven Dwarfs* (1937) and *Pinocchio* (1940) were reviewed in modernist literary magazines.

The modernist ambivalence about readers – wanting to be popular, yet disdaining mainstream culture – also haunted modernist fiction writers. Many of Hemingway's and Fitzgerald's writer characters live in fear of selling out and becoming 'hack' writers. At the other end of the spectrum, James Joyce and D. H. Lawrence both faced obscenity trials for shocking readers with the graphic sexual content in their novels. Writing of alienated, self-conscious modern men and women trapped in their own minds, Joyce, Faulkner, and Virginia Woolf all faced criticism for the difficulty of their radical experiments in stream of consciousness style, yet all became influential, international leaders in modernism. By 1950, Faulkner, like many other modernists, was awarded the Nobel Prize for Literature, and these literary revolutionaries became the established professors, critics, editors, and reviewers that the next generation would need to topple.

POSTMODERN AND CONTEMPORARY PERIOD 1950–PRESENT

Our contemporary period in literature begins after World War II as writers attempted to make sense of a nuclear-armed world. In many ways, these writers carried on the concerns of modernism – the inability to find truth, the alienation from an increasingly technological society, the confusion over the meaning of mass culture. While the modernists responded to those challenges with experimentation, however, many postmodernists feared that all possible experiments had been tried. Once-rebellious modernists now taught the next generation in university creative writing departments, and the new generation fought to find original literary forms that were not just derivative of earlier styles.

For postmodern writers like Tom Stoppard, Italo Calvino, Thomas Pynchon, Martin Amis, and Don DeLillo the way to reinvent literature is to dismantle it and expose its underlying structures. They mix genres and incorporate visual, digital, and audio media as well, as in Ntozake Shange's *for colored girls who have considered suicide/when the rainbow is enuf* (1977), which she calls a 'choreopoem'. Postmodern writers employ strategies like metafiction in which the writers disrupt the text to debate or discuss the way texts are written, and they question the dividing lines between 'high culture' literature and popular or mass culture content and forms – though even these techniques also appear in earlier novels, such as those by Henry Fielding (*The History of Tom Jones, A Foundling*, 1749), Laurence Sterne (*The Life and Opinions of Tristram Shandy, Gentleman*, 1759–1767), and Thomas Carlyle (*Sartor Resartus*, 1836). Taking the modernist uncertainty about truth and originality to new extremes, postmodern writers question the human ability to make sense of reality and the past. They often write about a world filled with commercial messages and advertising language marketing false identities to ourselves. Postmodern films like *V for Vendetta* (2005) and *Fight Club* (1999) exemplify these concerns.

Although not all writers of this period experiment with specifically postmodern stylistic techniques, most contemporary writers share this distrust of universal truth and emphasize the multiple truths revealed by looking at the world from outside the mainstream perspective. For many writers from marginalized cultural groups, this period's challenge to authority raised awareness of diverse literary traditions and welcomed diverse voices into the literary canon. Women writers (Sylvia Plath, Adrienne Rich, Elizabeth Bishop, Angela Carter, Margaret Atwood, Jeanette Winterson, Zoe Heller, and A. S. Byatt), writers of colour (Alice Walker, Ralph Ellison, Maxine Hong Kingston, Leslie Marmon Silko, Sherman Alexie, Toni Morrison), multicultural and immigrant writers (Philip Roth, Hanif Kureishi, Frank McCourt, Monica Ali, Jessica Hagedorn, Sandra Cisneros), counterculture and working class writers (John Braine, Allen Ginsberg, Jack Kerouac, Irvine Welsh, Anthony Burgess), and many others (Robert Lowell, Ian McEwan, John Updike) have made the contemporary period a time of increasingly free exploration of what constitutes a life. They have expanded definitions of literature and the 'literary' and radically revised our conventional understanding of history and accepted truth.

POSTCOLONIAL AND GLOBAL LITERATURE 1901–PRESENT

In many ways, the writers of either postcolonial or global literature of the twentieth and twenty-first centuries are also modernists, postmodernists, and contemporary authors. W. B. Yeats, James Joyce, Jorge Luis Borges, and Rabindranath Tagore were all intimately connected with other modernist circles of writers and artists, and they published in the same magazines and presses. Salman Rushdie and V. S. Naipaul employ many postmodern literary strategies, including metafiction. Both postcolonial and global writers today share the contemporary period's distrust of authority and a single source of truth, but this group particularly targets the authority of national identity and culture.

In her book *Born Translated: The Contemporary Novel in an Age of World Literature*, Rebecca L. Walkowitz (2015, p. 4) identifies a segment of recent literature that not only is produced in multiple translations and circulated globally almost immediately, but also integrates translation within the writing 'as a thematic, structural, conceptual, and sometimes even typographical device' for the multilingual speakers or narrators who choose one or more languages within the text. In the Argentine Borges's 'The Garden of Forking Paths' (1941), for instance, the main character, Dr Yu Tsun is a Chinese professor of English working as a German spy in the First World War. While chased by an Irish captain in the British military, Tsun meets Dr Stephen Albert, a British scholar of Chinese literature and culture who has discovered and read the famous novel of Tsun's ancestor. The entire story was originally written in Spanish, though presumably all of the characters would speak to each other in English; the tangle of transnational allegiances and connections further unmoors readers from any single geographical ground and orients the text on a global field.

J. M. Coetzee's *Waiting for the Barbarians* (1980) achieves a similar effect by refusing to identify any place names within the novel. Coetzee, a native South African who grew up speaking both English and Afrikaans, has lived in South Africa, England, the USA, and now Australia. In Coetzee's novel, the magistrate, the unnamed protagonist in *Waiting for the Barbarians*, lives at the rural edge of the Empire, where nomadic groups of the indigenous people, 'barbarians', still live just beyond the reach of the Empire's oppressive hand. Outside the walls of the outpost lie the ruins of an ancient village whose artifacts the magistrate collects and attempts (unsuccessfully) to read. The entire text offers a meditation upon the impossibility of cross-cultural communication, but it creates these effects by translating them into the blank space of a fictional landscape.

By reading these postcolonial and global literatures within a literary period that begins when the Victorian period ends, we can trace additional similarities in literary techniques and content that unite texts produced in the context of decolonization, anti-imperialism, postcolonial nation-building, cosmopolitanism, transnationalism, and globalization. We can recognize the emergence of 'Global Englishes', versions of the English language divorced from the national culture of England or the USA and adopted and adapted for communication in different local contexts worldwide (e.g. Spanglish, Hinglish, Chinglish). We can also recognize the cultural impact of educational and publishing industries that require students and writers to use English in order to reach wide audiences and gain wider recognition.

As a field, postcolonial literature emerges from cultures 'affected by the imperial process from the moment of colonization to the present' (Ashcroft *et al.*, 1989, p. 2). In this sense, Irish writers under the imperial rule of England from the sixteenth century through the twentieth or American colonial writers in the eighteenth century also produce postcolonial literature, but in general, the term is used to highlight the boom in writing from Africa, Asia, Australia, Latin America, the Caribbean, Canada, the Pacific islands, and First Nations in the Americas that began in the early twentieth century as an assertion of identity and difference, a recognition of value in culture and place, and, in many cases, a demand for independence.

For earlier generations of anti-colonial and postcolonial writers like Aimé Césaire, Léopold Sédar Senghor, Chinua Achebe, Gabriel García Márquez, Wole Soyinke, Anita Desai, Athol Fugard, Naguib Mahfouz, Seamus Heaney and Derek Walcott, writing in imperial languages (French, Spanish, and English) was a double-edged sword – both empowering them to convey their messages and criticisms of imperialism to the colonizing cultures and negating their sense of identity and ability to express themselves except through the language of imperialism. Writing in the languages of their native countries was likewise a political act of cultural-assertion as well as a risk of losing audiences or remaining unheard. By underscoring the pluralities of cultures and languages within a single colony or empire and exposing the arbitrary natures of governments and political borders, postcolonial literature erodes the links between language and nation that romantically guided earlier literary study and periodization under the assumption that a nation's culture finds a perfect expression in its official or standard language.

For newer, postcolonial generations born or raised after independence movements succeeded, the realities of transnational lifestyles have prompted new ways of writing about characters that are not rooted in a single place yet have not broken free of the cultural, racial, and social allegiances and prejudices that stem from inequalities among nations. Their texts also exist in a transnational publishing industry which does not require them to remain connected with a particular national literary tradition, but even prepares simultaneous translations in multiple languages and releases global texts (see Walkowitz 2009). Identifying these contemporary writers (Zadie Smith, Coetzee, Khaled Hosseini, Jamaica Kincaid, Bharati Mukherjee, Kazuo Ishiguro, David Mitchell, and Junot Diaz) with a transnational literary tradition highlights the transnational way we read and produce literature today.

LITERARY MOVEMENTS

Periodization of literature relies upon both literary and cultural factors for defining key characteristics. Those factors help readers identify the broad contextual trends surrounding the texts we analyse. In addition, we can focus on smaller literary trends created by communities of writers working cooperatively to shape *literary movements*. A literary movement is like a political or activist movement led by a group or groups of individuals with stated aims, but these aims focus on the meaning, purpose, and forms of literature. Some movements expand to subsume their periods as Romanticism did, but some, like Dada or surrealist movements within the modernist period, or Language poetry or the Black Arts Movement within contemporary literature, reflect particular subgroups of writers with explicit goals and methods of their own. These literary movements create cultural institutions which promote particular writers while others remain obscure due to lack of support. Knowing how texts relate to particular literary movements can productively add context to literary analysis.

For example, William Carlos Williams's 12-line 'The Red Wheelbarrow' poem describes a wheelbarrow, rain, and chickens (1986, p. 224). It appears in many anthologies of literature and is often taught in schools due to its basic vocabulary and simple structure. But what does it mean? Try to do a close reading, and the text teases readers with apparent symbols that the poem gives no key to decode. When we consider the text's literary context, however, the meaning becomes much easier to interpret. Williams is a modernist poet, embracing experimental techniques aimed at changing the way we read and write literature. The wheelbarrow poem first appeared in the immediate context of Williams's *Spring and All* (1923), a combination of prose, poetry, criticism, theory, manifesto, and art. The poem begins part XXII of the text, but does not stand alone; instead, it flows seamlessly into a prose discussion of categories and divisions that announces, 'The fixed categories into which life is divided must always hold' (Williams 1986, p. 224). In this context, the poem is not about wheelbarrows, but about the nature of poetry itself and the line breaks that distinguish poetry from prose. It is a poem about poetic experimentation.

Furthermore, Williams was not discussing such experimentation alone. In his early career, he belonged to the imagist literary movement, a community of writers centred upon Williams's poet friends Ezra Pound and H.D. The three met in Philadelphia when Williams and Pound were at the University of Pennsylvania and H.D. was preparing to attend Bryn Mawr. In Pound's 1913 essay, 'A Few Don'ts by an Imagiste', he emphasizes the need for free verse in modern poetry, but notes that the rhythm and line breaks must be purposeful, warning, 'Don't imagine that a thing will "go" in verse just because it's too dull to go in prose' (Pound 1913, p. 203). Similarly, H.D. (1916, p.19) touts the benefits of breaking, shattering, and dividing in 'Sheltered Garden' when the speaker calls upon the wind to rip apart the weak and pretty plants of the sheltered garden and make way for a new, powerful and modern beauty to take their place. As a contribution to this literary movement, Williams's text takes on new meaning. The wheelbarrow does not evoke a quiet day on the farm. The poem divides the 'wheel / barrow' across lines of **verse** in much the same way H.D.'s poem breaks tree branches and flower stems in order to explain what poetry can and should do to readers (Williams 1986, p. 224).

CULTURAL CONTEXTS

While literary history may help expand our analysis of artistic effects on meaning, cultural history can enhance our interpretation of the text's social significance. Cultural contexts range from the national to the local level and help to determine the value, status, and power of writers and the texts they produce. Cultural context can include the raw materials of culture that make their way into literature in the form of specific details of historical events and institutions (as in the *Mansfield Park* example above), or it can more generally designate the relative marginality or centrality of characters and writers and the effects of that social position on the meaning of texts. When a character or writer echoes the voice of mainstream culture, the meaning of the text shares that cultural authority. When a character or writer speaks from a position of *otherness* (being different from and marginal to the dominant culture due to race, class, gender, religion, disability, sexuality, ethnicity, or other social divisions), the text poses a challenge to mainstream readers and conventional values; its meaning carries at least some measure of countercultural dissent.

Analyse the impact of this cultural context on the meaning of the popular *Twilight* series (Meyer 2008). In it, the quiet and shy Bella Swan is caught between two supernatural groups. The vampires are wealthy, sophisticated, educated, beautiful, and nearly all are white. The shape-shifting wolves are Native Americans who live without many luxuries on a reservation. At first the outsider Bella maintains a strong relationship with the outsider wolves, but the books slowly integrate her into the family and power structure of the wealthy vampires, finally transforming her into a graceful, sophisticated, and powerful vampire who leaves behind her working class roots.

Without cultural context, we might analyse the books as a commentary on the conflict between unnatural, immortal power and natural, animalistic unity with the environment. Bella's emotional strength and the birth of her human-vampire child offer to redeem the cold, self-absorption of vampire-kind, while Bella is empowered with confidence and sexuality that can overcome her previous feminine weakness. With cultural context, however, the books are less revolutionary, sharing much more in common with *Mansfield Park* or Dickens's *Great Expectations* (1861) than with contemporary feminist literature. With the cultural context of race, class, education, and gender, Bella's transformation into a vampire compares to Fanny Price's eventual marriage into the family at Mansfield Park (Austen 1814). Bella's vampiric powers parallel the social power she gains by marrying into a higher class.

Despite the extraordinary appearance of supernatural creatures, the *Twilight* series ultimately offers little to challenge readers' values or to upset the cultural status quo. The text is easy, the style readable, and the genre predictable, because the writer does not need to find new language to express new meanings and views of the world. The text confirms accepted reality, and its language repeats accepted expressions of that experience. For writers and characters that do not enjoy the same status and values as their readers, their texts must employ strategies to communicate the reality of their differences. Analysis of such strategies may reveal meanings that question the foundations of their cultures.

Two major strategies, appropriation and abrogation, can explain many of these acts of cultural resistance in literature. *Appropriation* takes language, plots, styles, and genres from the dominant culture and twists them to meet other needs. We see this strategy often in political activism when one group embraces the names given it by their opposition and thereby disarms the criticism. In literature, appropriation appears in Angela Carter's revisions of fairy tale endings in which her women characters are not helpless victims. Appropriation is a constant theme in V. S. Naipaul's use of British and American authors to tell the story of Indian characters. In *Half a Life* (Naipaul 2001), Willie Somerset Chandran (named for Somerset Maugham) is the child of a loveless cross-caste marriage during the Indian independence movement. Throughout the text, Willie creates fictitious accounts of his life by appropriating common narratives of India. As he matures, he writes stories for his British missionary school teachers in India, for his classes in a London university, for BBC radio, and ultimately for a British press. None of the stories offers authentic truth. Instead, he mixes the narrative Somerset Maugham wrote about his own father, the style of Ernest Hemingway's short stories, the plots of Hollywood movies, and vague descriptions of the settings around his home in India in order to provide his British audiences exactly what they expect to hear. Willie's appropriations allow him to blend superficially into British culture, but readers of the book know his stories are lies and that Willie is slipping between the cracks of Indian and British identity, belonging to neither culture. Naipaul's strategies upset mainstream desires for clear and simple cultural labels. The text demonstrates that the truth about Willie and India lies only in the much more complicated story glimpsed between the lines.

Writing as a free African American in the nineteenth century, Frederick Douglass (1845) makes similar moves in his autobiography. In a time when African American slaves were not legally acknowledged as human, Douglass attempts to balance the goal of exposing the atrocities of slavery and condemning the institution while maintaining the good will of his white abolitionist readers. He does this by appropriating the language of Christian virtue and the values of freedom and education described in texts by white writers. Citing the arguments in favour of human rights he reads in a collection of classic speeches, Douglass (1845, pp. 39–40) credits *them* with giving 'tongue to interesting thoughts of my own soul, which had frequently flashed through my mind, and died away for want of utterance'. Appropriating their passion, Douglass uses their arguments as an excuse to express his own more radical and direct condemnation of slavery. Douglass (1845, p. 40) states, 'The more I read, the more I was led to abhor and detest my enslavers'. In this way, he avoids being accused of inappropriately criticising white Americans; he appropriates their own speeches to make the criticisms.

Indeed, much of Douglass's narrative politely and deferentially uses appropriation to ease his audience into an understanding of his experience under slavery and his efforts to escape it. Occasionally, however, Douglass also employs *abrogation*, the rejection of standard usage of the dominant language, in order to show his readers the utter difference between freedom and slavery that free citizens cannot fully imagine. Douglass (1845, p. 15) even cautions his readers that they have misinterpreted the songs sung by enslaved people, calling it a 'mistake' to read them as signs of happiness. Instead, Douglass (1845, pp. 13–14) describes the 'wild songs' as 'rude and apparently incoherent', filled with 'unmeaning jargon', yet through the sound, 'if not in the word', they convey the pain of 'the dehumanizing character of slavery'. What words could not explain, Douglass notes, the paradoxical songs did by creating new ways to combine strength, survival, beauty, dignity, and captivity.

Read without attention to context, this passage may seem designed merely to evoke pity for the slaves who remain in worse circumstances than Douglass. Indeed, it does. But contextual analysis enriches that meaning. When we recall the text's cultural context – produced by a former slave from the South, published for abolitionists in the North – the warning about misinterpretation carries added weight. The narrator, too, does not want his text misread as a sign of contentment with his own freedom. By combining appropriation with these moments of abrogation, the text attempts to show that ending the whippings is not enough, educating slaves is not enough; nothing short of complete freedom and equality will end this sorrow beyond words.

By recognizing the relationships between literature, history, language, and culture, we enable our literary analyses to address the layers of meaning that take place beyond the artistic and creative aspects of texts.

REFERENCES AND FURTHER READING

Ashcroft, B., *et al.* (1989) *The Empire Writes Back: Theory and Practice in Post-Colonial Literatures*, London and New York: Routledge.

Austen, J. (1814) *Mansfield Park: A Novel in Three Volumes*, London: T. Egerton.

Besserman, L. (ed.) (1996) *The Challenge of Periodization: Old Paradigms and New Perspectives*, New York: Garland.

Douglass, F. (1845) *Narrative of the Life of Frederick Douglass, an American Slave*, Boston: Anti-Slavery Office.

Eagleton, T. (1996) *Literary Theory: An Introduction*, 2nd ed, Minneapolis: University of Minnesota.

H.D. (1916) *Sea Garden*, London: Constable and Company.

Hayot, E. (2012) *On Literary Worlds*, Oxford and New York: Oxford University Press.

Machiavelli, N. (1998) *The Prince*, trans. H. C. Mansfield, Chicago: University of Chicago.

Meyer, E. (1897) *Machiavelli and Elizabethan Drama*, Weimar: Verlag von Emil Felber.

Meyer, S. (2008) *The Twilight Saga Collection*, New York and Boston: Little, Brown.

Midnight in Paris. (2011) Film. Directed by Woody Allen. [DVD] Culver City, California: Sony Pictures Classics.

Naipaul, V. S. (2001) *Half a Life*, New York: Knopf.

Pound, E. (1913) 'A Few Don'ts by an Imagiste', *Poetry*, vol. 1, no. 6, pp. 200–206.

Underwood, T. (2013) *Why Literary Periods Mattered: Historical Context and the Prestige of English Studies*, Burbank, CA: Stanford University Press.

Walkowitz, R. (2009) 'Comparison Literature', *New Literary History*, vol. 40, pp. 567–582.

Walkowitz, R. (2015) *Born Translated: The Contemporary Novel in an Age of World Literature*, New York: Columbia University Press.

Williams, W. C. (1986) *The Collected Poems of William Carlos Williams, vol. 1*, ed. A. W. Litz and C. MacGowan, New York: New Directions.

COMPARATIVE ANALYSIS

By digging deeply into the details and **context** of the language and cultural materials embedded within literature, we can use the tools of literary analysis to understand how an individual **text** works and why it works that way, but reading literature in isolation overlooks the relationships among different texts that contribute further to their meanings. Modernist poet and **critic** T. S. Eliot (1921, p. 44) cautions, 'No poet, no artist of any art, has his complete meaning alone … . [Y]ou must set him, for contrast and comparison, among the dead' who have established the literary tradition of the past. In this passage, Eliot calls for comparison with the **classic**s to determine which texts are truly original and to evaluate individual **author**s against their measuring stick, but comparison can expand literary analysis in several other ways as well.

In fact, comparison is one of the essential critical thinking strategies employed in any act of analysis:

> Comparison is a mode of thinking ... that seems fundamental to human understanding and creativity and that depends upon principles of relation and differentiation. Not just a cornerstone of analytic thought, comparison pervades everyday life as one of the ways in which we organize and make sense of the world around us.

> (Felski and Friedman 2013, pp. 1–2)

Put simply, we compare in order to know. If similar items and experiences behave similarly, we can use them to predict rules and patterns. Applying comparative strategies to literature, we can compare many texts by a single author to identify changes or continuities throughout his or her career. We can compare texts within a single **literary period**, **movement**, or **genre** to gain a deeper understanding of the larger category to which they belong (see discussion of William Carlos Williams, H.D., and the imagist movement in Chapter 3, 'Analysis in context'). Or we can compare across cultures, periods, genres, locations, and/or times

- to answer enduring questions about literature;
- to trace the influence of various literary traditions upon each other;
- to identify counter-traditions (e.g. women's literature, Irish literature, African American literature) that do not fit nicely into existing period- and nation-based divisions, and
- to assess the effect of different perspectives upon the way literature represents life.

This last, fundamentally humanist, sense of comparison drives the field of *comparative literature* which studies the relationships among world literatures in their original languages and in translation in order to 'make connections across traditions, boundaries, and identities' (Felski and Friedman 2013, p. 2). Such comparisons also complement the wide range of texts that most readers encounter – from popular culture films and television to literary classics of the past millennia, from contemporary literature emerging as the dominant voice of our time to obscure literary finds. As readers, our own reading histories establish the baseline for our analytical comparisons. The more diverse those histories, the more wide-ranging the comparisons that may inform our interpretations of literature.

Viewing comparison from a writer's perspective in 'Tradition and the Individual Talent', Eliot (1921, p. 44–45) sees literature in developmental terms as the writers of the present are 'directed' by the past, while the overall shape of past tradition is 'altered' and 'readjusted' when new literature calls our attention to particular genres, styles, themes, and content. For Eliot, each 'individual talent' contributes to the progress of literature by redrawing its outlines, but this process functions in readers in far less linear ways. Readers encounter texts out of chronological order and often unhampered by the hierarchies that Eliot describes, and each new text resonates with others they have read, 'altering' and 'readjusting' our views of literature and calling forth new meanings. Comparative analysis exposes these relational meanings.

If we analyse two poems by English Renaissance writers, published just 50 years apart, we can see the comparative effect on the meanings we identify. In 1557, Sir Thomas Wyatt (1831, pp. 18–19) published 'The Lover Despairing to Attain unto His Lady's Grace Relinquisheth the Pursuit', more commonly referred to by its first line 'Whoso List to Hunt, I Know Where Is an Hind'. The poem uses a conventional Petrarchan sonnet form to describe an unattainable love. The lover is one metaphorical hunter among many who may wish to find a deer (the lady). As the speaker of the poem, this lover exploits the repeated rhymes of the first octet (eight lines of verse) to convey the contradiction of his enduring desire for his beloved (the prey) against his exhaustion with the chase. Long pursuit has left him 'wearied … so sore', he follows only faintingly and 'leave[s] off therefore' (Wyatt 1831, p. 18). The new set of rhymes in the sonnet's second half announces a shift away from the lover. The final sestet (six lines of verse) serves as a warning to other hunters and a reminder to himself of the deer's inaccessibility: she wears a collar identifying her as 'Caesar's' and not to be touched by anyone else (Wyatt 1831, p. 19).

William Shakespeare's (1609, p. 37) Sonnet 87, similarly exposes the emotions of a lover giving up an unattainable beloved who is 'too dear for my possessing'. Read without the Wyatt sonnet, the logic of the speaker's repeated farewells to the beloved of higher status than himself culminates in the resigned conclusion of the final lines:

> Thus have I had thee, as a dream doth flatter,
> In sleep a king, but waking no such matter.
> (Shakespeare 1609, p. 37)

The relationship ends as the lover's dream of being worthy of his beloved is savoured, yet crushed in the last two lines. Like Wyatt's speaker, he has relinquished a love that is too good for him.

Compared directly, the latter poem confirms and reinforces the tradition of the unworthy lover represented in the first sonnet, yet the open logic of the second poem contrasts the emotional entrapment of the tight rhymes in the first. Unlike the two-part structure of Wyatt's poem, Shakespeare's sonnet uses three quatrains (four lines of verse) and a couplet (two lines of verse) with nine different sets of rhymes. Where Wyatt's speaker was caught between only two possible rhyming sounds ('hind' and 'sore') signalling his desire and his disappointment in the sonnet's initial octet, Shakespeare's speaker has far more options, and the rhymed pairs *possessing-releasing* and *deserving-swerving* make it unclear if the lover is being jilted or doing the jilting. Is it he or she who possesses then releases, he or she who swerves? Certainly, the speaker announces that his beloved is too good for him and that the gift of herself she gave him in the past '[c]omes home again' to her as they part. But is he admitting his unworthiness in the face of a far more valuable suitor, as Wyatt's speaker does, or is he flattering her in order to manipulate her into thinking she ended the relationship? In this case, the comparison of the two poems highlights the straightforward sincerity of Wyatt's speaker and the far more ambiguous calculations of Shakespeare's. As we read them together, they both amplify the **generic convention**s of the love sonnet form and remind us that the speakers draw upon conventions that could be manipulated in an attempt to woo (or release) their beloveds. Comparative analysis allows us to find new meanings within the relationships between the two texts.

COMMON THEMES

While some comparisons expose differences in meaning, others demonstrate the ways in which literature uncovers enduring questions that cross time and space and transcend the differences between and within cultures. By comparing across differences, we learn more about our human similarities through literature's common themes, such as love, death, loss, coming-of-age, war, journey, quest, freedom, freewill, fate, justice, relationships among people, the relationship between humans and nature, the relationship between the human and the divine. Comparative analysis allows us both to identify such themes and to examine their detailed applications.

A comparative focus on a single theme can lead our analysis beyond the logic and values of one time and place. The epic journey of the young wizard in J. K. Rowling's *Harry Potter* series (1997–2007) shares common themes with myriad other literary heroes. For example, there are many good reasons to compare Harry Potter with the young King Arthur. The main characters in both *Harry Potter* and *Le Morte d'Arthur* face dramatic magical encounters in infancy. Before he can walk or speak, Harry survives a magical attack by an evil wizard, leaving him orphaned and physically scarred (Rowling 1997). Arthur is conceived when King Uther Pendragon deceives Lady Igraine by magically impersonating her husband (Malory 1889). Both babies are separated from their families: Harry's parents are killed on the night of the attack; Arthur's father dies within a few years. Both are raised unaware of their magical pasts by less powerful families, where they are overshadowed by their older 'brothers' and secretly observed by wizards who plan to shape their futures. Later, both prove their rightful places – Arthur as king, and Harry as a member of the good wizards' Gryffindor House – by drawing out a sword from a stone in Arthur's case and a hat in Harry's (Rowling 1998). In both texts, the journeys begun by innocent young boys turn into complicated quests that reveal the moral dilemmas of those mired in a struggle for power. Following a common quest pattern, including dangerous travels, passage to a dark world guarded by terrible creatures, deception by mesmerizing tricksters, and ultimately a battle against temptation to achieve self-knowledge, both of their **narrative**s contribute to a longstanding literary inquiry about the exercise of power and how to draw the line between virtuous heroism and abuse.

Paired with Charles Dickens's *Oliver Twist* (1839), *Harry Potter*'s coming-of-age themes leap to prominence. Stripped of magical content, Harry's early childhood is only slightly better than Oliver's. Harry lives with his aunt and uncle who treat him as a servant. Oliver's birth to a fleeing woman who sought shelter in a workhouse before her death sweeps him up into the workhouse system where he is exploited, overworked, and chronically underfed by large, dull men much like Harry's uncle. The boys must both develop their personalities and maintain their innocence and good nature within these climates of abuse. They succeed with the help of kind patrons (Professor Dumbledore and the Weasleys for

Harry, and Mr. Brownlow and Miss Rose Maylie for Oliver) who swoop in just as the boys reach puberty. More importantly, Harry's and Oliver's self-sacrificing mothers transfer to their sons an inherited strength and goodness that no circumstance can quench – not even the vengeful schemes of evil wizards or Oliver's half-brother and rival heir.

The coming-of-age theme the two texts share, therefore, derives from another common theme: maternal love. In both cases, the texts offer examples of troubling, ungenerous mother figures who contrast with the idealized, true mothers of the boy's infancies. Their mothers' unconditional, selfless love animates and empowers the boys with a goodness that even strangers recognize and strive to protect. Although this force is unmagical in *Oliver Twist*, its charm works as well as the loving act of Harry's mother, which Rowling (2013, p. 736) calls 'ancient magic … that flows in your veins to this day'. Through these thematic similarities, both texts debate the role of inborn, inherited characteristics in shaping their heroes' coming-of-age.

TRANSLATION, VARIATION, REPETITION, AND REMIXING

As in the previous examples, thematic comparisons do not require any direct connection among the texts; messages they share are enough to justify comparative analysis. Nevertheless, literature is not produced in isolation, and often deeper connections do undergird our comparisons. From direct **allusion**s to characters, lines, titles, or plots of other texts to indirect echoes of past language, literary structures, images, or themes, no text stands completely alone. Literature is 'intertextual'.

In literary studies, the concept of **intertextuality** recognizes that even from the earliest written literature, texts are produced in dialogue with each other, whether intentionally or not (see Kristeva 1980). Literary critic Linda Hutcheon (2006, p. 2) reminds us that much 'art is derived from other art; stories are born of other stories … retold … in new forms'. Today, most writers will gladly list the authors who influenced them most. Indeed, Rowling lists Dickens among the authors she believes all children should read (Higgins 2006), but she calls attention to *David Copperfield* (1850) with its private school plotlines, not to the orphaned characters in *Great Expectations* (1861) or *Oliver Twist*. Her omissions do not limit our ability as readers and literary analysts to notice the threads of Oliver's and Pip's lives within Harry's. As Eliot implies in 'Tradition and the Individual Talent', those threads extend in both directions at once, and later works alter our perceptions of those that preceded them. Identifying intertextual relationships reveals additional layers of meaning that accrue both in new texts and in the earlier ones with which they are intertwined. Furthermore, recognizing the intertextuality of texts written or released at the same time offers an important analytical view of the context that produced them all.

Intertextuality is at work whether an author explicitly quotes another text or whether the connections are purely coincidental – whether the author has read the original text or not. For instance, an author may never have read or seen Shakespeare's *The Tragedy of Romeo and Juliet* (first published in 1597), but pervasive cultural references to the young lovers have made their names synonymous with romantic passion and impulsive devotion. Even Romeo's name contains within it intertextual resonances with the words 'romance' and 'Roman'. When our hypothetical author names a character Romeo, he or she may not intend to allude to lines from the famous balcony scene where Romeo declares his love for Juliet nor to the tomb scene of their final deaths, but the ghosts of those textual details still arise with every repetition of Romeo's name (Shakespeare 1997b). If the new text also mentions a rose, readers aware of Romeo's famous speech about Juliet's name will inevitably connect the two. That is intertextuality.

Intertextuality can appear in the direct use or parody of quotations, allusions, characters' names, or plot lines. It can also appear indirectly in response to a particular genre or literary movement, an often-used image, or a typical character or archetypal plot (e. g. star-crossed lovers, rival siblings, heroes with a tragic flaw). The indirect forms operate subtly and remind us of the complicated interrelationships among texts, relationships that can be created by writers who produce texts or by readers who use and interpret them.

The realities of intertextuality, as well as the desire to make literature more widely available to different audiences in different times, have made translations, variations, remixes, and repetitions of literature quite common today. Translations convert literature from one language to another or from one audience to another, such as children's versions of classic adult literature. Variations and remixes can be seen in fan fiction, prequels, sequels, mashups, and reboots like the *Star Trek* and *Terminator* film franchises. Common mashups of literary classics and zombies abound, while texts like Alan Moore's 1999 comic books of *The League of Extraordinary Gentlemen* or Caryl Churchill's play *Top Girls* (1982) lift multiple, recognizable characters from literature and history out of their original contexts, set them on intersecting paths, and imagine the results. The most elaborately constructed intertextual forms, *adaptations*, offer repetitions with a difference. Through adaptations, we enjoy familiar stories with a creative twist that can cross media, genres, settings, contexts, modes of narration, or points of view. In *A Theory of Adaptation*, Hutcheon (2006, p. 7) defines the form as 'an announced and extensive transposition of a particular work or works', meaning that adaptations make it clear which source text they are repeating and then carry out their adapted repetition to its logical end.

For example, many adaptations of literary classics have shifted the focus from male to female characters, such as Jane Smiley's adaptation of *King Lear* told by Goneril (Ginny) in *A Thousand Acres* (1991) or Margaret Atwood's transference of the story of *The Odyssey* (Homer 1996) from the husband to the wife. In *The Penelopiad*, Atwood (2005) not only places new value on Penelope's perspective but grants her a voice and asserts that a woman who stays at home can generate her own dramatic content as well.

Adaptations like these have been popular for ages. Atwood herself (2005, p. xiv) acknowledges that Odysseus's story was already subject to repetition and variation in ancient times: 'Mythic material was originally oral, and also local – a myth would be told one way in one place and quite differently in another'. Taking a cue from such variations, Atwood relies upon multiple sources for her adaptation of Homer's text. The end result is a story of equal cleverness and scheming, but this time told from Penelope's side. Commenting on the goal of adaptation, Hutcheon (2006, p. 4) notes that readers enjoy it for the 'comfort of ritual combined with the piquancy of surprise. Recognition and remembrance are part of the pleasure (and risk) of experiencing an adaptation; so too is change'. The surprise of Penelope's bold defiance of her husband makes Atwood's adaptation especially exciting and new for twenty-first century readers.

Comparing the representations of Penelope, Odysseus, their house-hold servants, and the gods across *The Penelopiad* and *The Odyssey* may offer new insights into the complexity of ancient Greek culture and into our own society's generalizations about ancient and modern life.

TRANSLATION

When applying the strategies of comparative analysis in order to interpret intertextuality, readers can approach translations as highly specialized forms of adaptation. In translations, a multilingual reader/writer attempts to convey in a new language the content, style, and meaning of a source text. The translator may work closely with the original author or may make the translation without any guidance, perhaps even long after the original writer's death.

Fundamentally, translation aims to share texts with readers who could not understand them in their original language. Many of the texts referenced in this book are English translations of world literature, and the ready availability of translations into dozens of world languages since the mid-twentieth century has opened global audiences to a vast array of cultural and historical perspectives and expanded our understanding of literary history. In 1816, John Keats (2007, p. 12) wrote about the tremendous potential of translation to expand readers' ways of thinking. The poem 'On First Looking into Chapman's Homer' celebrates the speaker's experience of reading Homer's *Odyssey* recounted in English. He distinguishes between the summaries he had heard of the poem and its poetic text rendered in translation by George Chapman. Having studied Latin but not Greek, Keats relied upon the English translations. In the poem, the speaker describes this new access to classical literature as the opening of a pass across mountains or the discovery of a new planet, figuratively allowing him to enter a new world (Keats 2007, p. 12). Significantly, Keats's title stresses the adaptive nature of translations. He looks into 'Chapman's Homer': neither an entirely original poem by Chapman, nor Homer's unchanged text. As Keats acknowledges, translation produces an intertextual end product, combining the creative efforts of both authors and the cultural influences of both contexts.

Translation studies in the field of literature have attempted to understand this complicated relationship between the original and the translation (see Apter 2006, Benjamin 1996, Shields 2013). Traditionally, comparative analyses of translations focused on authenticity and the faithful recreation of one language's literature in different words. Translators and their readers must weigh the relative values of translating literally to convey the sense and content of the original against figurative translations aimed at reproducing the experience, tone, connotations, cultural significance, and style of the source text.

Given these difficulties, translation has been the subject of wide interpretive debate. On one hand, translation bridges cultures and nations, holding out the promise of a cosmopolitan understanding of local conditions beyond our own geographic borders and an appreciation of those elements of human nature that pervade the whole world. On the other hand, translation can reproduce power differences between nations and cultures. For instance, Stieg Larsson's *Män Som Hatar Kvinnor* (2005) is known worldwide as *The Girl with the Dragon Tattoo*, though its Swedish title means 'men who hate women'. When the book series hit the bestseller lists in the USA and the United Kingdom in 2008, the English translation usurped the original. Although a highly-acclaimed Swedish-language film adaptation was released in 2009, the dominance of English-speaking audiences almost immediately prompted an English-language film adaptation with an American director and English-speaking cast. In some ways, then, the translation expanded global connections between Swedish culture and the cultures of those who have read the text in 40 different languages. In other ways, the English translation overtook all others, smoothing out cultural differences (like the title) and appropriating a great story to meet its own cultural needs. Our comparative analyses of translated texts can address these cultural effects that extend beyond linguistic differences.

Whether or not the translator emphasizes his or her role in creating a new text, translations multiply the meanings within the originals and translations as they involve multiple cultures, multiple authors, and, of course, multiple readers. Former US Poet Laureate Robert Lowell called his collection of poetic translations *Imitations* (1962) and included translations of poems from Greek, Russian, French, German, and Latin languages, despite his lack of fluency in all of them. For Lowell, the act of translation was its own form of comparative analysis and a sign of productive dialogue among texts and writers. Lowell even dedicated his famous translation of Charles

Baudelaire's 'To the Reader' to Stanley Kunitz, author of an alternative translation of Baudelaire's poem (Baudelaire 1955, p. 3).

ANALYSING ADAPTATION

Given the great boom in adaptations into film, poetry, novels, graphic novels, musicals, plays, video games, and other media today, literary analysis can benefit from this fruitful area of creative comparison. For instance, when William Shakespeare (1997a) first published *The Tragedy of Hamlet, Prince of Denmark* in 1603, the most pressing questions facing Hamlet centred on maintaining the order of the kingdom in a time of generational transition and unrest spreading far beyond Denmark's borders. Hamlet makes the speeches, Hamlet sets the traps, and Hamlet is crushed beneath his ghostly father's command to avenge his death by killing the new King Claudius. In 1967, the widespread tragedy with that familiar story also shone a spotlight on the many minor characters who were entangled in the plots of Hamlet and King Claudius and who suffered as casualties in their power plays. Adapting Shakespeare's Elizabethan tragedy into a postmodern, absurdist play, Tom Stoppard (1967) shifted the focus to Hamlet's friends and the dilemma of playing supporting roles in someone else's story. Stoppard's *Rosencrantz and Guildenstern Are Dead* depicts the lives of the characters who are only summoned into being when the play *Hamlet* refers to them. They have no self-knowledge, no memory, no history, no purpose beyond that mentioned in passing by Shakespeare's characters. They are driven to deliver their scripted lines when cued to enter the stage, but between scenes, they live suspended between the drama's events and the real world. In this limbo, they attempt to understand their experiences and fear that they may be mere fictions. The adaptation brilliantly repeats Shakespeare's own lines about actors and plays, but turns the hierarchy of power and value upon its head. Stoppard makes readers mourn the loss of Shakespeare's pawns and calls into question the meaning of the great destruction within the original play.

When Stoppard adapted his play into a film in 1990, the shift in genre led to additional changes in meaning. While the play evokes a self-referential sense of the blank limbo of characters waiting in the wings for their cues to call them back to the stage where *Hamlet* is being performed, the film fills in these off-stage spaces with alternative landscapes and settings, anachronistic props, and surreal sound effects that both suggest the possibility of another life for the characters and make that life disorienting and disconnected from any particular time and space. More than in the play, the film makes it seem that Rosencrantz and Guildenstern are already dead and attempting to patch together a semblance of their lives from scattered memories in an afterlife world.

By adapting the play into different genres (prose and lyric poetry respectively) both John Updike (2000) and Natasha Trethewey (2002) offer creative adaptations of *Hamlet*'s characters that suggest new meanings and new ways of understanding the texts' claims to reality and truth. Updike's novel *Gertrude and Claudius* writes the stories of Hamlet's mother and stepfather in long, narrative form. Focalized alternately on the perspectives of Gertrude and Claudius (see **narrative** and narrator in Chapter 2, 'Close reading: words and forms'), the novel expands their backstories, telling of Gertrude's pre-marriage concerns about King Hamlet, her strained relationship with Prince Hamlet, and her adulterous affair with Claudius. The long, novelistic preamble to the play's actions absolves Gertrude of all guilt for her husband's death, even partially excuses Claudius's betrayal, and sets the characters on their fatal paths as Claudius attempts to win over the moody Prince Hamlet. The final chapter of the novel overlaps with the royal procession in act 1, scene 2 of the play, including quotes from Claudius's and Gertrude's speeches along with an omniscient narrator's revelations of their unspoken thoughts and motives. Comparative analysis of the two texts calls into question the violence of Hamlet's reactions to his mother and to Ophelia and can open up new interpretations of the ghost of King Hamlet's virtue and motivations in both the novel and the play.

A looser adaptation of *Hamlet*'s character of Ophelia appears in Trethewey's *Bellocq's Ophelia*. This poetry collection does not follow the plot of Shakespeare's play; Trethewey's adaptation even avoids an entirely tragic end. Yet Trethewey's Ophelia, a light-skinned African American in early twentieth-century New Orleans, Louisiana, both embodies many of the other Ophelia's characteristics and questions the emphasis that has been placed on her role in Shakespeare's play. As Hamlet's love interest, Shakespeare's Ophelia is caught between the powerful attractions of a prince, the maternal interests of a queen, and the ambition and obsequiousness of her own father, a royal advisor. Throughout the play, her father both cautions her against an unequal relationship with Hamlet and advises her to hold him at a distance to encourage Hamlet into making a legal commitment to her. She is valued by her family and Hamlet's for her ability to draw the attention of the kingdom's heir, and that attention results in her father's death and her own suicide. In the play, she has little opportunity to express her own desires and continually responds passively to the actions and motivations driving the other characters.

Performers of the play often seek out Ophelia's role for the scenes just before her death when she appears as a beautiful and broken woman, singing irrationally in her grief over her father's loss while deferentially presenting the queen with flowers. It is a scene so picturesque that it and her later off-stage death have been recreated in art and literature hundreds of times. The artistic renderings of Ophelia's death are the subject of Trethewey's title poem, a layering of the play and the art that have glorified the image of the dying girl. Instead, 'Bellocq's Ophelia' looks at the body and face of a real woman in an early twentieth-century photograph by E. J. Bellocq (Trethewey 2002, p. 3). In the photographed woman, the poem's speaker sees defiance, resistance, and a desire to speak. The poetic adaptation demands comparison with Shakespeare's Ophelia by turning away from the description the messengers give of her death and instead highlighting the complex and at times accusatory words she embeds in her rhymes and songs.

For readers, analyzing the intertextual meanings between the play and the poem enriches, renews, and revitalizes the four-hundred-year old character. By investigating the differences produced by changes to context, perspective, genre, media, and language, comparison keeps both literature and its interpretations alive and fresh.

REFERENCES AND FURTHER READING

Apter, E. (2006) *The Translation Zone*, Princeton, NJ: Princeton University Press.

Atwood, M. (2005) *The Penelopiad*, Edinburgh: Canongate.

Baudelaire, C. (1955) *The Flowers of Evil*, eds. Marthiel and Jackson Mathews, New York: New Directions.

Benjamin, W. (1996) 'The Task of the Translator', in M. Bullock and M. W. Jennings (eds.) *Selected Writings Volume 1 1913–1926*, Cambridge, MA, and London: The Belknap Press of Harvard University Press.

Dickens, C. (1839) *Oliver Twist*, London: Richard Bentley.

Eliot, T. S. (1921) *The Sacred Wood: Essays on Poetry and Criticism*, New York: Knopf.

Felski, R. and Friedman, S. S. (eds.) (2013) *Comparison: Theories, Approaches, Uses*, Baltimore, MD: Johns Hopkins University Press.

Higgins, C. (2006) 'From Beatrix Potter to *Ulysses*... What the Top Writers Say Every Child Should Read', *The Guardian*, [Online] 31st January. Available from: http://theguardian.co.uk. [Accessed 22nd May 2015].

Homer (1996) *The Odyssey*, trans. R. Fagles, New York: Penguin.

Hutcheon, L. (2006) *A Theory of Adaptation*, New York: Routledge.

Keats, J. (2007) *Selected Poems*, ed. J. Barnard, New York: Penguin.

Kristeva, J. (1980) *Desire in Language: A Semiotic Approach to Literature and Art*, ed. L. S. Roudiez, New York: Columbia University Press.

Larsson, S. (2005) *Män Som Hatar Kvinnor*, Stockholm: Manpocket.

Malory, T. (1889) *Le Morte d'Arthur: Sir Thomas Malory's Book of King Arthur and of His Noble Knights of the Round Table*, ed. W. Caxton and H. O. Sommer, London: David Nutt.

Rowling, J. K. (1997) *Harry Potter and the Philosopher's Stone*, London: Bloomsbury.

Rowling, J. K. (1998) *Harry Potter and the Chamber of Secrets*, New York: Scholastic.

Rowling, J. K. (2013) *Harry Potter and the Order of the Phoenix*, London: Bloomsbury.

Shakespeare, W. (1609) *Shake-speares Sonnets*, London: Thomas Thorpe.

Shakespeare, W. (1997a) *The Tragedy of Hamlet, Prince of Denmark*, in G. B. Evans and J. J. M. Tobin (eds.) *The Riverside Shakespeare*, Boston: Houghton Mifflin.

Shakespeare, W. (1997b) *The Tragedy of Romeo and Juliet*, in G. B. Evans and J. J. M. Tobin (eds.) *The Riverside Shakespeare*, Boston: Houghton Mifflin.

Shields, K. (2013) 'Challenges and Possibilities for World Literature, Global Literature, and Translation', *CLCWeb: Comparative Literature and Culture* [Online], vol. 15, no. 7. Available from: http://docs.lib.purdue.edu/clcweb/ [Accessed 22nd May, 2015].

Stoppard, T. (1967) *Rosencrantz and Guildenstern Are Dead*, New York: Grove Press.

Trethewey, N. (2002) *Bellocq's Ophelia*, Saint Paul, Minnesota: Graywolf Press.

Updike, J. (2000) *Gertrude and Claudius: A Novel*, New York: Random House.

Wyatt, T. (1831) *The Poetical Works of Sir Thomas Wyatt*, London: William Pickering.

5

ANALYSIS AND THE CRITICS

Previous chapters have focused on types of literary analysis that can be performed directly upon literary texts either alone or in combination with each other. This chapter turns to the interpretations we make in dialogue with other readers and interpreters – analyses completed with the aid of **critics**.

In everyday use, a person who criticizes makes negative judgements, but in the field of literary analysis, a *critic* values, appreciates, and in many ways promotes literature by exploring textual details and discussing their meanings in public conversations. In the nineteenth century, readers, publishers, and fellow writers disseminated literary reviews in magazines and regular newspapers. The reviewers made understanding and evaluating literature a matter of public debate in much the same way as today's *New York Times* or *Guardian* episode recaps and reviews of *Humans, Mad Men, Game of Thrones* and other television favourites. Throughout the twentieth century, critics increasingly split into different groups. Popular critics continued to write reviews for consumers in newspapers and general magazines. Writers and editors reviewed literary techniques and debated new directions among the subscribers of literary magazines for insiders. Academic critics (like the many professional literary critics to whom this book refers) emerged from the growing field of English studies in colleges and universities. These scholars charged with increasing the knowledge base in literary studies produce expert criticism based on research and share their ideas with students and other experts through critical introductions to the literature, articles in specialized journals, and books published by university and academic presses. While these three main types of critics continue to operate today, the twenty-first century has jumbled and mixed these categories in fascinating ways. Through online venues, literary analyses by a wide array of critics – from world experts to lay critics who rate books on Goodreads or Amazon – are readily available at the fingertips of any smartphone user. The practice of reading now takes place within a larger community of interpretation that includes critics, teachers, **author**s, publishers, marketing departments, and fellow readers of all ages.

A single statement by a critic may be the key to analysing meaning, or it may lead to a consensus in interpretation that closes off all other possibilities. For example, in 1933, William Faulkner wrote an introduction to *The Sound and the Fury* (1929) which highlighted the importance of the scene when the family's only daughter, Caddy, climbs a tree to eavesdrop on the adults at her grandmother's funeral wake (Anderson 2007, p. 32). Faulkner later repeated this point in interviews about the novel, saying that he started writing *The Sound and the Fury* based on 'the picture of the little girl's muddy drawers, climbing the tree to look in the parlour window with her brothers that didn't have the courage to climb ... waiting to see what she saw' (Gwynn and Blotner 1965, p. 1). By identifying this account of the origin of the book, Faulkner – acting as a kind of self-critic – gives readers information they cannot ignore or erase as they attempt to find their own interpretations of the novel. Indeed, these comments are often used to introduce the novel in blurbs on book jackets, editors' introductions, and other critical guides. For any reader who encounters this critical statement, the image of Caddy's undergarments, muddied by playing at the stream earlier in the day haunt the whole text and filter Caddy's every attempt to gain freedom through that lens; she is not afraid to get dirty in every sense of the word.

The critic, in this case the author himself, has performed a significant role by calling attention to a detail that unlocks and shapes overall meaning of the text. A critic's most important purpose, however, is to advance the conversation about literature.

Consider how the interpretation of *The Sound and the Fury* might change if Faulkner had not used his authority to fix the meaning on Caddy. What if he had said the Easter sermon in the final section of the novel was the genesis of the whole narrative, or Mr Compson's gift of a watch to his son Quentin (Faulkner 2012)? Would we see the novel as a journey towards redemption or a ticking time-bomb of disaster as the characters march into the complications of modern life? What if Faulkner had said nothing and left the interpretation to his readers, as most writers like to do? All of these meanings, and many more, would remain available to readers of the text. Indeed, they do remain available in our own analyses, whether we read Faulkner's comments or not, and many critics have added their own interpretations to Faulkner's. The sections that follow demonstrate how any reader can participate in the critical conversation about literature.

ABOUT CRITICISM

Attempting to define **criticism** in an essay called 'The Function of Criticism in the Present Time', nineteenth-century writer Matthew Arnold (1865, p. 36) calls it '*the disinterested endeavour to learn and propagate the best that is known and thought in the world*'. This is a rather tall order, but Arnold was writing in a time when criticism meant merely offering opinions based on taste about whether or not readers liked certain texts; he ambitiously (though not entirely successfully) aimed to create common standards to guide critics and to make their work more of a formal study than book club gossip. Today, the concept of criticism in academic circles is much more narrowly defined. *Criticism* applies the methods of literary analysis and close readings in order to expand our understanding of a particular text or texts.

First, we distinguish between book and film reviews and criticism. Although we use the common term 'critic' to describe writers of both, reviews mainly evaluate whether texts are good or bad with the ultimate goal of recommending the reading experience or warning others away from a text that is not worth it. In contrast, criticism makes evidence-based arguments about the possible ways to interpret texts and to uncover ever deeper and more complex meanings within them. Criticism may make value judgements, but no longer based on taste: criticism may evaluate the influence of texts upon each other, their contribution to innovation in literary practice, their impact upon readers and societies, but only if historical and cultural evidence or textual examples from close readings can support those judgements.

Second, the implications of critical arguments extend beyond recommendations for readers.

- Criticism may use analysis of texts in order to explain underlying truths about language or aesthetics.
- Criticism may work from textual examples to explore the role of story-telling, life-writing, self-expression, or political speech.
- It may have political or cultural aims to revise or refine our accepted knowledge about a particular culture, time period, or writer.
- It may recover buried knowledge by locating writers and texts that went out of print or fashion but made valuable contributions in an earlier time.
- Or it may expose the subversive and revolutionary content within literature in order to inspire people to change.

With the vast assortment of critical resources available free online, even casual readers have ready access to criticism in many forms. Any reader confused about a reference, symbol, or scene in a book can find snapshot summaries and analyses of most **canonical** literature in SparkNotes, Shmoop, Wikipedia, or myriad student study blogs. Readers can post questions on thousands of text or study sites and receive answers, complete with links to books and critical analyses online. Why did Voldemort try to kill Harry Potter as a baby? What is the meaning of the mockingjay in *The Hunger Games*? Why do the Schlegel sisters attend concerts in E. M. Forster's *Howard's End*? Which beach does Lydia visit in Jane Austen's *Pride and Prejudice*? A quick online search can not only answer the question but reveal the existence of multiple Web resources designed to track these answers. Nonetheless, the quality of such general criticism can be spotty at best. Although Web sites like these may offer useful clues to interpretation, they are largely unregulated and unedited except by their own users.

Academic criticism – criticism that is reviewed by experts prior to publication, edited and published with writers' and publishers' names and reputations attached to the work – offers more credible and more extensive interpretations. Academic critics generally have read every text published by the authors they study and quite a few others within that literary period as well. In addition, they, too, read the work of other critics, bringing that wealth of information to their extended literary analyses.

Search engines like Google Scholar and Bielefeld Academic Search Engine (BASE) help to limit search results to academic criticism that meets those criteria, but the best sources for locating criticism lie within research libraries where databases like the MLA International Bibliography sort out only academic journal articles and high quality books limited to the fields of language, literature, or film studies. Readers new to using and finding literary criticism in articles, books, or online sources should generally seek criticism from credible publishers within the fields of language and literature. For example, researchers investigating modernism for the first time may end up quite confused by articles from the fields of history, philosophy, economics, sociology, psychology, or even art due to the vast differences in definitions of the term 'modernism' among various disciplines. An art historian may begin modernism in 1860, while a political scientist may speak of modernism in the 1700s. Neither of their definitions will help to explain or contextualize the early twentieth-century period in literature characterized by experimentalism (see Chapter 3, 'Analysis in context'). For literary analysis, formal, academic literary criticism provides the best foundation.

READING CRITICISM AND IDENTIFYING CRITICAL DEBATES

Analysis can be improved by understanding what critics have already said about particular texts and which important ideas and questions experts continue to debate. Criticism written by literary scholars can be challenging to read due to their use of specialized jargon, literary terms (see Chapter 2, 'Close reading: words and forms'), and theories (see Chapter 6, 'Analysis and literary theory'). Like any genre, however, the critical article or book chapter follows its own **generic convention**s that can make reading criticism easier and more rewarding.

Critical arguments may not immediately state their claims. Often the first paragraphs offer an interesting anecdote or example of the kinds of issues the critic plans to discuss; these paragraphs may even describe a past argument only to reveal that the critic wishes to correct or reverse parts of that argument. Next, usually within the first five paragraphs, the critic explains the point of the argument. Either early in the article or within each of its subdivisions marked with subheadings, the critic outlines the major questions this research aims to answer in what is called a literature review of the critical conversation. Although the body of the essay may move deep into detailed examples, these overarching ideas are picked up again in the conclusion which emphasizes what new knowledge or interpretations the critic adds. Certainly, academic critics break conventional rules as often as writers of any other sort, and many articles could serve as exceptions to these guidelines. For readers approaching criticism for the first time, however, knowing the common places to look for a thesis or research question in an academic article can help unlock the valuable insights that criticism can provide.

To illustrate the way academic criticism works, we will turn to the critical conversation about Jane Austen's *Pride and Prejudice* (1813). Since the 1990s, this novel about the complex and contradictory courtship of Elizabeth Bennet and Mr Darcy has been adapted into popular culture through dozens of films, ranging from period pieces, like the 1995 BBC miniseries with Jennifer Ehle and Colin Firth or the 2005 film starring Keira Knightley, to loose, intertextual derivatives, like *You've Got Mail* (1998) starring Tom Hanks and Meg Ryan. The popularity of these adaptations has made even non-readers familiar with Austen's characters and plot. The novel employs a comedy of manners to establish Elizabeth's prejudice against Mr Darcy for what she sees as his excessive pride and disdain for what he views as her family's lack of manners and status. Despite these first impressions, they find themselves drawn together through the interwoven relationships of Elizabeth's sisters and Darcy's former and present friends until they finally realise their misjudgements and declare their love for each other.

Surveying both recent and foundational criticism about *Pride and Prejudice*, we can see several common trends. Much of the criticism reflects on the way the novel both develops narrative strategies and the novel genre and at the same time discusses reading practices through the characters within the text (Wootton 2007, Bonaparte 2005, Moses 2002, McCann 1964, Halliday 1960). Various contextual analyses of gender roles, family structures, marriage, and the economics of inheritance also serve to highlight the novel's social dimensions (Macpherson 2003, Hudson 1989, Koppel 1989, Newton 1978).

Many critics, like William Deresiewicz (1997, p. 503) begin their analyses with a close reading of the famous first line of Austen's novel, announcing the compulsory nature of marriage for men of wealth. In 'Community and Cognition in *Pride and Prejudice*', Deresiewicz (1997, p. 504) compares this line to the opening of other Austen novels and observes the unusual absence of the main character from this novel's first paragraphs. From there, he argues that the text waits to introduce Elizabeth Bennet because the narrative is ultimately more interested in the way her 'community thinks, talks, exerts influence' upon her, and through its communal values creates Elizabeth's identity. Turning against other critical characterizations of Elizabeth as independent and empowered, Deresiewicz (1997, p. 504) casts a critical eye on the community's judgements of Darcy and other characters in order to claim that the real story is about Elizabeth's 'struggle to wake herself out of a community in which she is all too comfortably embedded'. We can use the argument within this article to further trace the conventions of academic criticism.

After the detailed discussion of the novel's opening line and a literature review of the critical conversation that emphasizes Elizabeth's intelligence and difference from the rest of the community, Deresiewicz announces his thesis about community and spends the bulk of the article supporting that claim with detailed close readings. The article is broken up into three sections under the following subheadings: 'Cognition and the Single Woman', 'The Pleasures of Density', and 'Friendly Fire' (Deresiewicz 1997, pp. 504, 511, 520). Analysing the logic of judgement displayed in various conversations among characters, Deresiewicz asserts in the first section that Elizabeth's community allows for no individual thought. With the community's dependence upon consensus of opinion created through conversation, the characters make quick judgements based on general beliefs rather than carefully reasoned explanations of the events they observe. In this way, Deresiewicz explains the almost instant agreement about Darcy's pride among the entire community, including Elizabeth, despite the text's characterization of her as set apart from everyone else. The second section goes on to demonstrate the ways in which Elizabeth derives pleasure, comfort, and identity within the dense interrelationships that keep the community in sync: 'That she is a mocker of convention is central to the image she projects ... [but] she could not stand apart from the group were she not standing firmly within it' (Deresiewicz 1997, p. 513). Indeed, the critic argues, that tight-knit community makes it possible for Elizabeth to get to know men as friends and to exercise her independence in making decisions; it also allows Austen to produce a novel that 'transforms the process of courtship as she found it in her novelistic predecessors' (Deresiewicz 1997, p. 519).

The article's final section turns to the way the text manages to free Elizabeth from her community's condemnation of Darcy's pride by forcibly separating her from friends, family, and neighbours − both by communicating privately with Darcy in letters and by transporting her far from home. Through such separation, the critic argues, Elizabeth can exercise individual judgement and can draw rational conclusions based on evidence, not received wisdom and communal values. For Deresiewicz, the novel's and Elizabeth's progressive acts lie in revising the meaning of social conventions by rejecting full integration within a community. Instead, Elizabeth and Darcy create what Deresiewicz (1997, p. 530) calls an 'imagined community' of only the friends and family members who are not too foolish or improper to join them in their new home where 'the marriage assumes many of the functions of a community in the strict sense'. No longer content to stand out among her tight-knit community, Elizabeth will stand away from it, allowing only certain members of her earlier circle to participate in her new, aristocratic life. In drawing this conclusion, the critical article weaves together debates about gender and marriage with a cultural critique of community and analysis of the early nineteenth-century novel form. The critic inserts himself within those three lines of criticism and combines them to offer a new understanding of the radical and yet not too subversive portrait of culture *Pride and Prejudice* provides.

CRITICAL RESPONSE

In expanding our own analyses based on critical conversations, we must balance the trends and topics discussed by scholars with our own original contributions to what is known and understood about a given author or text. We must respond to the critics. This section will offer an extended example of the process for building an analysis in dialogue with the critics.

Just as Deresiewicz does in his article, we must identify the trends, then ask: Are the critics overlooking something? Does the critical conversation align with our own close readings of the most interesting parts of the text? Are there ways that different critical arguments could be combined to arrive at new interpretations?

For example, the critical conversation surrounding *Bride and Prejudice* (2004), one of the many film adaptations of Austen's novel, centres upon the dramatic cultural differences between the two texts. Directed by Gurinder Chadha, who also made *Bend It Like Beckham* (2002), the film considers the complex ties of family, education, and economy that span the United Kingdom, the USA, and India. Tracing the transnational marriages of different members of the South Asian diaspora, *Bride and Prejudice* transforms the marriageable Bennet daughters into the Bakshis of Amritsar in contemporary India. Will Darcy is the American heir of a US-based, international luxury hotel conglomerate. His best friend from his college years at Oxford, Balraj (Mr Bingley in Austen's novel), is a London barrister from a prominent Delhi family. Balraj and several other characters could be described as hybrid, meaning they blend together multiple cultures, or transnational, meaning their international lives and experiences leave them identifying with multiple places at once, transcending the limits of a single national identity. During the course of the film, the characters travel from Amritsar to Goa, London, New York, Los Angeles, and back again for courtships and marriages as they map the travels of Austen's characters upon a global stage. The film also reflects its multicultural content in its style. The English language script and international cast place the film among other globe-trotting romantic comedies like *Love Actually* (2003), while the musical infusion of song and dance in the Bollywood tradition of the Indian film industry offers conventions for presenting romantic relationships that are as stylized as Austen's own dances and balls. The film is playful and funny, filled with song-and-dance numbers as well as almost ridiculous missteps and misunderstandings in dialogue.

The main trends in criticism about *Bride and Prejudice* identify the similarities and differences between Bollywood conventions and the nineteenth-century novel of manners. Critics like Cheryl A. Wilson (2006, p. 323) call the two genres 'well-suited partners' that can 'preserve and update the cultural critique' in Austen's original novel. In the film, critics note that the social critique targets gender, class, and neo-imperialism embodied both in Darcy's family's hotel chains and in Mrs Bakshi's repeated comments about moving to the USA for economic gain (Vogt-William 2009, Mathur 2007).

The most pointed critical debate stems from the transnational and hybrid forms of character identities and filmic genres *Bride and Prejudice* creates. Sabine Nunius (2010) and other critics question whether the South Asian characters can maintain authentic identities within British and American contexts and, likewise, whether the film's cultural concerns about preserving what it calls 'real India' can be understood in the unreal exoticism and consumerism of a Bollywood-Hollywood mix (*Bride and Prejudice* 2004). On one hand, Elena Oliete-Aldea (2012, p. 167) argues that the transnational film transcends 'cultural boundaries based on prejudice and uneven power relations' as its allows both characters and audiences to share their pride and delight in multiple national and cultural spaces, ranging from Amritsar's Golden Temple and Goa's beaches to Los Angeles's Hispanic neighbourhoods, California's deserts, and the London Eye. On the other hand, Tamara Wagner (2011, p. 105) warns that the film achieves that transcendence by repeating stereotypes of Indian exoticism; the film's ironic use of the Bollywood genre in songs like 'No Life without Wife' does not 'escape' such stereotypes, but rather 'internalizes' them in a 'distorted' representation of India's cultural identity. For Wagner, *Bride and Prejudice* may attempt to eliminate prejudice, but it does not succeed.

Based on a review of this critical conversation, one question remains: Is this film, which is aimed at Western audiences, critiquing Eurocentric views of India through its satire of cultural prejudices, or is it surrendering to them by showing a comedic blending of cultures that reinforces Western economic and social dominance?

To add our own answer to this critical question, we must offer a new analysis of the details of the film. In this case, returning to the source of the film's adaptation can offer some solutions to our interpretative problem. As an adaptation of Austen's novel, *Bride and Prejudice* must find a way to create barriers of misunderstanding between Darcy and Elizabeth (named Lalita in the film), then, through gestures of loyalty to Lalita's family, Darcy must overcome those barriers. In Austen's novel, there is never any question as to

Elizabeth's attractiveness, and Darcy admits his love for her quite early in the text. The same is true for Darcy and Lalita in *Bride and Prejudice*. The obstacle for Austen's Darcy lies in setting aside his dislike of Elizabeth's family and friends, or more precisely her class status that is lower than his own. In contrast, Elizabeth must overcome the insult she feels in being put down due to her class. Only once she can be assured that her marriage will not replicate their differences in social position does she accept his proposal. As Deresiewicz (1997, p. 530) points out, at the end of the novel Elizabeth and Darcy create their own 'imagined community' where they live surrounded by people who will help them forget their social differences and enjoy their private attraction to each other without the intrusion of questions of public status or identity.

Deresiewicz's idea of the 'imagined community' offers a model of analysis that we can apply to *Bride and Prejudice* as well. For Darcy and Lalita, community-based and culture-based prejudices drive a wedge between them from the start – despite their instant romantic and physical attraction to each other. Darcy lives in the USA and has never visited India before; he tries to make sense of the experience based on stereotypes and received communal views (fearing 'Delhi belly' from eating the food, for instance). Lalita, too, sees Darcy through a communal lens. She distrusts the American outsider who seems too interested in work to appreciate his visit. She fears that he wants only to exploit India for business, harming or erasing India's culture in the process. Their initial, communal-minded views of each other prevent them from forging a personal relationship.

Over the course of the film, Darcy and Lalita forge a connection beyond the barriers of their prejudices and, in the end, get married in India. But what of their imagined community? Do they overcome power differences or does Darcy just carry Lalita away to the USA where she will always feel her difference, her otherness, among Darcy's family and friends? The evidence of the film suggests that they can establish an equal relationship (despite his wealth) and can success-fully build a cross-cultural, transnational community for themselves, in part because they already live transnational lifestyles. Together the characters traverse tens of thousands of miles over the course of the film, and they show every sign that such travel is a regular occur-rence. Their easy passage through global spaces suggests that they already frame their lives as individuals, not as members of exclusive, or exclusionary communities. For example, in the opening of the film, Balraj, who now lives in London, comments on his enjoyment of what Darcy sees as the 'mayhem' and 'bedlam' of Amritsar, characterizing it as 'a bit like New York' (*Bride and Prejudice* 2004). Likewise, Lalita's mother enjoys the idea of her daughter going abroad to marry, saying, 'we could visit her any time' (*Bride and Prejudice* 2004).

Darcy's position is even less grounded in conventional community. Reflecting on his upbringing, Darcy reveals that his own family has a transnational lifestyle, commenting that the only reason his parents remained married was because 'they lived in separate countries' (*Bride and Prejudice* 2004). Darcy's mother may be firmly American, but the family she has created is rootless and global. Lalita meets them not in their home, but in one of their many hotels. Unlike Darcy's Pemberley estate in Austen's novel, *Bride and Prejudice* offers no stable home for Will Darcy, and the final marriage in Amritsar acknowledges that there is no other appropriate community to which he could return.

Similarly, for Lalita, her community includes her family and friends from Amritsar, but throughout the film, one friend moves to the UK, another relocates to Los Angeles, and her sister is poised to migrate to London with Balraj. Two major musical numbers refer to these transplanted identities with lines about 'overseas brides' and flying away 'from Amritsar to UK' (*Bride and Prejudice* 2004). Significantly, these moves are not described as losses. In the song 'Marriage Has Come to Town,' the first transnational friend is called 'the golden girl / the centre of the world' (*Bride and Prejudice* 2004). This idea of an individual centre contradicts the rigid cultural divisions that threaten the relationships throughout the film, and it shows that *Bride and Prejudice* can be understood as paralleling *Pride and Prejudice*'s move away from community to individuality.

In a new interpretation of the film, we can spotlight the importance of the most transnational spaces of all – the airplanes and helicopters. Through conversations up in the air above the national and cultural borders that divide them, Lalita and Darcy find ways to break down their prejudices and unite. Their imagined community is flying between the multiple locations, friends, and family they adore. Of course, this solution is unrealistic. It depends upon Darcy's wealth and line of hotels to maintain their fully transnational life, but the film is a fantastic romantic comedy built upon the foundation of an earlier romantic comedy with an impossibly wealthy and attractive bachelor who must find a bride. The genre dictates a happy ending, not realism. Its most interesting cultural contribution lies in its ability to establish a large set of spaces in which Darcy and Lalita's happiness can be sustained.

Thus, our engagement with the critical conversation enables us to draw new conclusions and to find new meanings in the details of the film. We can use comparative analysis, close readings, and contextual analysis to understand and support these interpretations. By increasing our awareness of other critical analyses of the texts we read and films that we see, we can enrich our own analyses and add our own interpretations to the public discussion of literature.

REFERENCES AND FURTHER READING

Anderson, J. D. (2007) *Student Companion to William Faulkner*, Westport, CT: Greenwood Press.

Arnold, M. (1865) *Essays in Criticism*, Boston: Ticknor and Fields.

Austen, J. (1813) *Pride and Prejudice: A Novel in Three Volumes*, London: T. Edgerton.

Bonaparte, F. (2005) 'Conjecturing Possibilities: Reading and Misreading Texts in Jane Austen's *Pride and Prejudice*', *Studies in the Novel*, vol. 37, no. 2, pp 141–161.

Bride and Prejudice. (2004) Film. Directed by Gurinder Chadha. [DVD] USA: Miramax, 2004.

Deresiewicz, W. (1997) 'Community and Cognition in *Pride and Prejudice*', *ELH*, vol. 64, no. 2, pp. 503–535.

Faulkner, W. (2012) *The Sound and the Fury*, New York: Modern Library.

Gwynn, F. L. and Blotner, J. (eds.) (1965) *Faulkner in the University: Class Conferences at the University of Virginia 1957–1958*, New York: Vintage Books.

Halliday, E. M. (1960) 'Narrative Perspective in *Pride and Prejudice*', *Nineteenth-Century Fiction*, vol. 15, no. 1, pp. 65–71.

Hudson, G. A. (1989) 'Sibling Love in Jane Austen's *Pride and Prejudice*', *Persuasions*, [Online] vol. 11. Available from: http://www.jasna.org/persua sions/ [Accessed 22nd May 2015].

Koppel, G. (1989) '*Pride and Prejudice*: Conservative or Liberal Novel – or Both?' *Persuasions*, [Online] vol. 11. Available from: http://www.jasna.org/persua sions/ [Accessed 22nd May 2015].

Macpherson, S. (2003) 'Rent to Own; or, What's Entailed in *Pride and Prejudice*', *Representations*, vol. 82, no. 1, pp. 1–23.

McCann, C. J. (1964) 'Setting and Character in *Pride and Prejudice*', *Nineteenth-Century Fiction*, vol. 19, no. 1, pp. 65–75.

Mathur, S. (2007) 'From British "Pride" to Indian "Bride": Mapping the Contours of Global Postcolonialism', *M/C Journal*, vol. 10, no. 2. [Online] Available from: http://journal.media-culture.org.au/0705/06-mathur.php [Accessed: 22nd May 2015].

Moses, C. (2002) '*Pride and Prejudice*, Mr Collins, and the Art of Misreading', *Persuasions*, [Online] vol. 23. Available from: http://www.jasna.org/persuasions/ [Accessed 22nd May 2015].

Newton, J. L. (1978) '*Pride and Prejudice*: Power, Fantasy, and Subversion in Jane Austen', *Feminist Studies*, vol. 4, no. 1, pp. 27–42.

Nunius, S. (2010), 'Exoticism and Authenticity in Contemporary British-Asian Popular Culture: The Commodification of Difference in *Bride and Prejudice* and Apache Indian's Music', in R. Emig and O. Lindner (eds.) *Commodifying (Post)Colonialism: Othering, Reification, Commodification and the New Literatures and Cultures in English*, Amsterdam, Netherlands: Rodopi.

Oliete-Aldea, E. (2012) 'Gurinder Chadha's *Bride and Prejudice*: A Transnational Journey through Time and Space', *International Journal of English Studies (IJES)*, vol. 12, no. 1, pp. 167–182.

Vogt-William, C. (2009) 'Transcultural Gender Interrogations in *Bride and Prejudice*: Intertextual Encounters of the South Asian Diasporic Kind', in M. Meyer (ed.) *Word and Image in Colonial and Postcolonial Literatures and Cultures*, Amsterdam, Netherlands: Rodopi.

Wagner, T. S. (2011) 'Foreign Fantasies and Genres in *Bride and Prejudice*', in L. Lau and A. C. Mendes (eds.) *Re-Orientalism and South Asian Identity Politics: The Oriental Other Within*, London and New York: Routledge.

Wilson, C. A. (2006) '*Bride and Prejudice*: A Bollywood Comedy of Manners', *Literature Film Quarterly*, vol. 34, no. 4, pp. 323–331.

Wootton, S. (2007) 'The Byronic in Jane Austen's *Persuasion* and *Pride and Prejudice*', *The Modern Language Review*, vol. 102, no. 1, pp. 26–39.

6

ANALYSIS AND LITERARY THEORY

Outside the field of literary studies, the term 'theory' often means the opposite of 'fact'. In this sense, 'theory' is part of a continuum that also includes 'hypothesis' and 'guess'. In literary analysis (and most other academic fields), 'theory' means something else entirely.

Literary theory is the opposite of literary 'practice' or literary **criticism** which applies strategies of analysis in order to make interpretations of particular texts. Literary theory addresses the abstract concepts behind analysis: our underlying assumptions about the nature and function of literature. With titles like *Theory of Prose*, *Aesthetic Function*, or *Gender Trouble: Feminism and the Subversion of Identity*, interpreting literature is not theory's goal. Theory aims to explain ideas, to clarify the complete meaning of prose, aesthetics, gender, or identity in order to enrich the conversations we have about those topics as we apply them within criticism. Thus, a critic may note that Joseph Conrad's *Heart of Darkness* uses the generic conventions of detective fiction only to reveal a mystery that cannot be solved (Brooks 1984), but a theorist would seek to explain the function of narrators in any novel and the relationship between detection and novelistic writing (Barthes 1975). Readers interested in analysing literature are not called upon to write theory, but they may find referring to theory productive and enlightening.

As a review of literary history demonstrates (See Chapter 3, 'Analysis in context'), the definition of literature and even the act of reading have changed over time. This means not only that literature is open to different interpretations when we read specific texts, but also that the point of literature itself is up for debate. Once we see that the way we approach a text changes the meanings we find within it, we have entered the realm of literary theory. In *Literary Theory and Criticism*, Patricia Waugh (2006, p. 2) states that 'literary theory insists that assumptions underlying reading practices must be made explicit, and that no reading is ever innocent or objective or purely descriptive'. Knowing different literary theories can identify and refine the set of assumptions that drive our passion for exploring texts, and it can furnish clear terms and concepts to describe those assumptions.

What do we mean by delineating our assumptions about reading practices? We mean that we do not take for granted the meaning of terms like reader, **author**, language, or **text**. We do not simply assume we know how literature represents the world or how fictional characters relate to reality. We take a step back – often even a step outside literary studies into psychology, anthropology, philosophy, history, economics, or other fields – to clarify precisely what we mean.

Writing in the 1970s about major changes happening in literary theory at the time, Roland Barthes (1977, p. 155) explained that new concepts in other fields of study or disciplines have brought change to literature as well:

> It is a fact that over the last few years a certain change has taken place (or is taking place) in our conception of language and, consequently, of the literary work.... The change is clearly connected with the current development of (amongst other disciplines) linguistics, anthropology, Marxism, and psychoanalysis.

In the years Barthes describes, new work in linguistics changed the way we look at the connection between meaning and words; anthropology changed the way we view conflict and inequality; Marxism changed the way we see the relationship between literature and economic systems; and psychology changed our views of the unconscious desires that reveal themselves in language. When we shifted our assumptions about words, cultures, work, and even our most

intimate thoughts and feelings, we likewise transformed our fundamental understanding of literature. In some cases, critics refer directly
to the books and articles from these other disciplines to establish
basic principles and concepts which they apply to literary analysis.
In other cases, **literary theorist**s (like Barthes) produce abstract
arguments directly about the nature of literature itself, including Barthes's own essay 'The Death of the Author' (see Chapter 1,
'Introduction: thinking about literature').

Sometimes a particular theoretical explanation (theory for short)
of some aspect of reading or writing practice will gain widespread
acceptance, and critics will operate under that shared assumption
for decades as they did during the boom in New Criticism and
Practical Criticism in the mid-twentieth century. At other times,
competing schools of theory rooted in opposing assumptions (e.g.
New Criticism v. New Historicism and Cultural Materialism) will
spark both critical and theoretical debates.

Theory gives us a way to understand how to approach a text and
how to make decisions about what matters and what it really means.
Reading the key texts of major schools of theory allows us to peek
behind the curtain of the courses we take, the critical articles we
read, and our own unexamined assumptions about literature.

EVERYONE HAS A THEORY

Whenever we approach a text, we make fundamental assumptions
about the value of literature and the literary elements we find most
significant. Whether we know it or not, we base our readings upon
those theoretical assumptions. In the 1960s, most secondary schools,
colleges, and universities taught literature following the assumptions
of New Critical or Practical Critical theories. By the 1980s and 1990s,
many high schools added or even switched to a focus on readers'
responses to literature, while colleges and universities have since
embraced theories based on culture, history, psychology, and language.
Students transitioning into higher education today are often surprised
by the dramatic difference in the way they are asked to read and talk
about literature. That difference can be explained by theory.

When we analyse, or even just read, a text, our assumptions and
values will call our attention to some details and cause us to dismiss
others as unimportant. For example, if we assume that understanding

how characters feel is of utmost importance, we may concentrate intently on dialogue but ignore descriptions of setting or action. Interpretations based on those assumptions would be very different from those we make if our primary interest focuses on nature and ecological values or questions of ability and disability.

We may not yet know those assumptions, but we can easily identify our interests within literature. We may inherently seek to understand conflict between power and the powerless. We may be drawn to questions of identity and the meaning of gender, race, class, and other cultural categories. We may find language itself most thrilling, may think of literature as a great escape into the creative space of romanticism or a complicated puzzle of linguistic meaning. We may like what literature reveals about human relationships and the human mind and the concept of the self. We may look at literature as an extension of natural creativity, exposing the interconnectedness of global ecosystems and integrating us within our natural world no matter where we live. We may be fascinated by the relationship between literature and cultural production, with consumers, marketers, and publishers influencing the literature that audiences can find. Recognizing these underlying interests, priorities, and values can reveal our assumptions and the theories with which we are already aligned.

In his overview of literary theory, Cornell University professor Jonathan Culler (1992, p. 204) identifies several conceptual issues that pervade literature:

> the relations between men and women; the most common and puzzling manifestations of the human psyche; the effects of material conditions, social organization, and political power on individual and collective experience; and the human and inhuman dimensions of the play of language and representation.

Given these broad literary subjects, Culler divides literary theory into several categories based on the questions it attempts to answer:

- *Defining the literary*: How does literature compare with 'nonliterary' texts? What makes a text 'literary'? (Culler 1992, p. 222)
- *Aesthetics*: How does literature work as a form of art interested in the nature of beauty and sensory experience? What is the purpose of literature's aesthetic elements? (Culler 1992, p. 223)

- *Language and representation*: What does it mean to represent the world in language? What is the 'nature of **representation**'? (Culler 1992, p. 218)
- *Identity and the self*: What does literature reveal about the nature of identity, humanity, and selfhood? (Culler 1992, p. 219)
- *Politics and culture*: What political effects does literature create, and does analysing literature lead to cultural change? (Culler 1992, p. 217)

Different literary theories address each of these questions by defining and redefining what literature is, how to read it, and which literary elements are most important. A brief history of the development of literary theory in the West before the twentieth century can demonstrate the effects of those theories.

Although the following writers did not define themselves as literary theorists, their ideas served as the foundation for literary theory by explaining the assumptions about the nature of literature in their time. In the classical period, Aristotle, Plato, and Longinus attempted to define literature and its effects on readers. Aristotle's (1997) *Poetics* addressed questions about the nature of representation (see 'Introduction: thinking about literature') and the structures and qualities of literary texts. He also offered the first formal analysis of literary **genre**s and terms, resulting in the celebration of some genres as great, 'noble' literary works and the demotion of other genres to merely light entertainment. During the medieval period, the focus of theory shifted from form and effect to meaning and interpretation. Medieval scholars developed the fields of hermeneutics and exegesis, and they theorized these processes in their efforts to analyse and interpret the Bible and other sacred texts (see Chapter 1, 'Introduction: thinking about literature').

The Renaissance brought an explosion of secular literary production, shifting away from the religious interests of earlier periods. Renaissance literary theory, like Sir Philip Sidney's 1595 essay, 'An Apology for Poetry', sought to defend the moral and philosophical influences of literature and refined the concept of literary representation as distinct from deception, fabrication, and imitation. Like the Renaissance writers before them, Neoclassical theorists in the seventeenth and eighteenth centuries returned to Greek and Latin sources as they approached definitions of aesthetic value and literary form.

French writers Pierre Corneille (1862) and Nicolas Boileau (1683) expanded upon classical concepts like the dramatic unities and poetic genres by applying principles of reason in the writer and pleasure in the reader to determine guidelines for maintaining balance and harmony in literature. In England, John Dryden (1668), heavily indebted to Corneille, advocated the use of judgement to balance imaginative 'fancy' and produce serious and artistic poetry, while Alexander Pope (1711, p. 42) upheld the values of genius, taste, and learning, tempered by nature and sense, as the means to produce poetry that could maintain 'Wit's Fundamental Laws'. Samuel Johnson's four-volume *Lives of the Most Eminent English Poets with Critical Observations on Their Works* (1781) reinforced many of these principles of balance, reason, nature, and beauty, while also codifying the **canon** of English literature that best represented those values.

The period of Romanticism ushered in a greater embrace of literary creativity and an emphasis upon the influence of literature in the world. William Wordsworth (1800, pp. xiv) famously linked literature to emotion, inspiration, and genius by calling 'good poetry… the spontaneous overflow of powerful feelings … by a man who being possessed of more than usual organic sensibility had also thought long and deeply'. For Percy Bysshe Shelley (1840, p. 5), this sensibility has the power to transform and guide society as 'the pleasure resulting from the manner in which [poets] express the influence of society or nature upon their own minds, communicates itself to others, and gathers a sort of reduplication from the community'. This belief in the unbounded power of literature to change its readers and its world fundamentally changed the purpose of reading and interpretation. In the Victorian period, the literary theories of Matthew Arnold and John Ruskin agreed that literature can influence the world, but not through emotions; they emphasized the role of good literature in promoting good morals, excellent taste, intellectual growth, and cultural unity and advancement. They distinguished 'low culture' writing which feeds our emotions and prejudices from 'high culture' literature which transcends humanity's more practical and baser tendencies. The majority of these early theories address the first three questions in Culler's list.

Since the beginning of the twentieth century, however, literary theory has become increasingly diverse and has devoted ever more energy to the questions of identity, selfhood, culture, and society. As the field has grown more interdisciplinary and international, it has also progressed in a less linear fashion. Ideas that emerged in the 1910s–1930s in Russia, Czechoslovakia (now the Czech Republic), France, Austria, Germany, Algeria, and Italy sometimes did not reach the wider field of literary theory until the 1960s or 1970s. As a result, some questions may dominate theoretical debates and their applications in literary criticism for a decade, then fall into obscurity, only to be revived when a new translation raises awareness of another theorist – even one from decades past.

A straightforward timeline of literary theory, therefore, cannot fully describe the different branches of the field. More thorough guides to literary theory (Bertens 2014, Waugh 2006) can help to untangle its complex historical development from 1920 to the present as well as to explain the detailed concepts and arguments associated with different theoretical schools. The paragraphs that follow will briefly introduce different types of literary theory and their key theorists based on the fundamental questions they address, though it is important to remember that many theories may offer answers to questions beyond their main area of inquiry.

THEORIES OF DEFINING THE LITERARY AND AESTHETICS

Combining a desire to determine the characteristics of literature (as opposed to other texts) with an interest in the transformative effects of aesthetics, *New Criticism* (Brooks 1947, Ransom 1941), *Practical Criticism* (Leavis 1933, Richards 1924), *Formalism* (also called Russian Formalism) (Shklovsky 1991, Propp 1968), and *Functionalism* or Czech Functionalism (Mukařowský 1970) seek universal truths about human morality and purpose arrived at through aesthetics and outline underlying rules that govern formal literary structures. As we have seen in our earlier examination of close readings (see Chapter 2, 'Close reading: words and forms'), New Critics and Practical Critics focused on the way the aesthetic elements of texts resolve profound paradoxes in thought and experience, creating a coherent meaning through literary language where scientific or practical language failed. The formalists and functionalists, too, were interested in aesthetic forms and effects, but their main goal was not to determine the meanings of individual texts; they sought to identify the source of the aesthetic dimension in literature as a whole. Therefore, they codified the differences between everyday language and the heightened, self-referential, and defamiliarized language found in literature (see Chapter 2, 'Close reading: words and forms'). Citing literary examples of language that calls attention to itself as language, the formalists and functionalists showed how literature shakes readers from a complaisant, unexamined use of words and forms into a state of perception and awareness. Functionalists and formalists as well both applied techniques of scientific observation and experimentation in order to study the decidedly unscientific effects and structures of literary language.

Although few critics continue to apply these theories wholesale into their analyses, these theorists developed methodologies for close reading and identified literary forms and terms that are still in widespread use today.

THEORIES OF LANGUAGE AND REPRESENTATION

From the 1920s onward, developments in the field of linguistics have led to many new theories of language, the medium of literature. Much as art history has debated the role of photography as art, wondering whether it merely captures existing reality or reshapes it through the processes of editing, cropping, selection, and transfer through technology, modern literary theorists look upon language with scepticism and challenge our reliance upon symbols, signs, and words to convey meaning transparently. Ferdinand de Saussure's *Course in General Linguistics*, first published in 1916 in France, radically reconceived the underlying rules of language by separating the word or sign into two parts: 1. the 'signifier', which serves as the outward symbol or 'sound-image' pointing to meaning and 2. the meaning, concept, or object being 'signified' (Saussure 2011, p. 67). By separating the word or sign into its component parts, Saussure (2011, p. 67) argues, we recognize that their connection is entirely 'arbitrary': no inherent properties of letters or sounds (signifiers) dictate that they should express certain ideas (signifieds). If the relationship between signifier and signified were not arbitrary, words like 'show' and 'snow' should have relatively similar meanings given the similarities between their signifiers. In fact, all languages ought to have arrived at similar sounds to express meanings if there were an innate connection between a signifier and its signified. Clearly, they do not. By making readers rethink the obvious, the transparent meanings of words they had taken for granted for so long, and asking readers to dig deeper into the laws used to govern meaning and its arbitrary signifiers, Saussure's theory spawned several literary theories: *structuralism* (Saussure 2011, Jakobson and Halle 1956), *structural anthropology* (Lévi-Strauss 1958), *semiotics* (Barthes 1972), and *deconstruction* (Derrida 1978, 1976). These theories were interested directly in questions of language and the possibility of understanding linguistic rules as they apply to literature, culture, signs, and texts of all sorts.

By rejecting essential meanings inherent within language and words, structuralists in both linguistics and anthropology identified the source of meaning in the interrelationships and differences among signs. They distinguished between the *parole*, the individual example of speech, writing or other uses of linguistic signs, and the *langue*, the regulated system of patterns for language and syntax that allow users to derive a shared sense of meaning from any given *parole*. Moreover, these structuralists named the different component units of the *langue* to establish reliable, universal rules for understanding those linguistic systems across cultures and historical periods. The common science fiction figure of the adventuring anthropologist whose knowledge of linguistics allows him or her to communicate with any new human tribe, no matter how remote, demonstrates the highest aims of early linguistic and anthropological structuralism.

Literary structuralism, narratology, and semiotics further apply the concepts of sign systems that are structured and ordered through difference by expanding their applications to units of narrative, literary genres, and even non-linguistic signs of culture, including rituals, clothing, gestures, food, consumer goods, and a variety of other objects. Such theories strive to make the seemingly infinite variety of signs meaningful and knowable, if not predictable, by offering binary systems into which they can be categorised and through which their interrelationships can be shown.

Unlike the other theories of language and representation, deconstruction does not provide reliable structures for knowing the world; as its name implies, deconstruction explodes and destroys such structures by exposing them as arbitrary as well (see 'Everything is a construction' below). Pioneered by Jacques Derrida, deconstruction agrees with the structuralists that there is no innate, essential meaning within language, but where structuralists attempt to escape that problem by elevating their analysis to the level of systems of language and other signs,

Derrida argues that such escape is impossible. For deconstruction, human knowledge exists only within language, a language doomed to produce slippery and inconsistent meanings. It is important to note that deconstruction does not negate all meaning, but questions any effort to locate meaning by ruling out or excluding certain truths. Deconstructionists assert that meaning can only be located among the free play of signs, where preconceived limits and prejudices embedded in our representations in language can be exposed, questioned, and bypassed in an effort to move ever closer to an elusive truth.

THEORIES OF IDENTITY AND THE SELF

Theoretical responses to questions about the nature of humans' sense of self and identity have produced several literary theories over the past century. Beginning with Sigmund Freud's *The Interpretation of Dreams*, published in German in 1899, twentieth-century theorists have ceased to view the human experience as consistent and continuous and literature as the seamless expression of a unified human soul. Built upon the assumption that the human mind is split between its unconscious and conscious awareness and desires, Freud's theory asserts that all of the content we repress from our rational, conscious experience remains in our unconscious mind; furthermore those unconscious desires, drives, and fears return to us through dreams and other linguistic and physical symptoms. In *The Interpretation of Dreams*, Freud (1913) analyses the words and images of his patients' dreams in order to uncover common unconscious desires that serve to define universal psychological forces and drives.

In perhaps his most famous application of dream analysis, Freud (1913, pp. 222–224) actually applies his techniques to literature, Sophocles's *Oedipus Rex*. Claiming that the myth of Oedipus 'originates in an extremely old dream material, which consists of the painful disturbance of the relation towards one's parents by means of the first impulses to sexuality', Freud (1913, p. 224) models a kind of literary analysis aimed at human psychology and focused on characters as well as authors and readers. Freud contrasts Oedipus's stated desire to avoid killing his father against the unknowing murder of his father and marriage to his mother. From this example and other cases of dreams about patricide and/or incest, Freud concludes that boys understand their gender identity in part by developing an unconscious desire to assume their father's role. For Oedipus in the play written by Sophocles, this repressed desire emerges in an exceptionally tragic and abhorrent way, but the example, Freud argues, offers a window into the collective human unconscious.

Throughout *The Interpretation of Dreams*, Freud makes both Oedipus and Shakespeare's Hamlet targets of his case studies, suggesting that the creation of literature shares much in common with the psychological process of dreaming. *Psychoanalytic literary theory* (Lacan 2007, Kristeva 1980) exploits these connections between the multiple meanings of language and the complexities of the conscious/ unconscious human mind in order to understand our role as *subjects* (as in the subject of a sentence, 'I') who construct our identities in language. In recent decades, literary theorists of *disability studies* (Davis 2013) have further challenged psychological and medical views of normalcy and abnormality, exploring the impact of mental and physical disabilities on the way literature represents and defines humanity.

Accompanying the psychological branch of literary theory, several social and cultural theories emerged throughout the twentieth-century to challenge assumptions about human differences, especially those relating to gender and sexuality, race, ethnicity, and nationality. It is worth noting here that despite the promise of freedom and human dignity championed in the Age of Enlightenment (see Chapter 3, 'Analysis in context'), up until the twentieth century human differences were almost universally understood as a dichotomy in which one group was superior to another, inferior one (often viewed as a different species): as history unfolded, Greeks saw themselves as superior to 'Barbarians', Romans were superior to Huns, Europeans were superior to Moors, Ethiopians, and 'Cannibals', men were superior to women, and 'civilized' people were superior to 'savages' worldwide. As Western cultures increasingly divided these groups into evolutionary categories, scientists, politicians, philosophers, and writers of earlier centuries simplified the variety of human cultures and appearances by deciding which groups were more 'advanced' and which 'backward'. Mapping differences onto inequality served to justify invasions of other nations, enslavement of other peoples, legal restrictions on those outside the dominant group, and the virtual erasure of the voices and stories of the people on the margins. Several twentieth-century theories sought to overturn these social hierarchies and to redefine human differences on more equal footing.

Early *feminist literary theory* sought to highlight the existence of women writers and to assert the value of women's experience which had been silenced by a literary establishment controlled by men. Redefining gender differences as the effect of cultural practices and power dynamics, not intellectual or physical limitations, feminist literary theory questioned women's second-class status in society and promoted women's literature (Woolf 1981, Beauvoir 1953) as the equal of literature by men. By mid-century, feminist literary theory began to expose the damaging literary representations of women that reinforced unequal gender roles in society (Gilbert and Gubar 1979, Showalter 1977). Today advocates of *gender theory* and *queer theory* also question assumptions about the fundamental nature of gender and sexuality, looking at masculinity, femininity, heterosexuality, and homosexuality and their relative social values as defined by culture, not as naturally confined to the bodies of certain people (Butler 1990, Irigaray 1985, Sedgwick 1985, hooks 1984, Cixous 1976). Feminist theory, gender theory, and queer theory also see gender and sex as a catalyst of literary narrative, arguing both that literature of the past has depended upon inequalities in gender and sex to produce literary genres and that literature of the future requires multiple voices to better align literature with political justice and cultural truth.

Theories of race and ethnic studies have adopted a similar mission and followed a similar trajectory. In the early twentieth century, writers of African descent throughout the diaspora argued for the value, equality, and accomplishments of the black cultural and literary traditions which white society had long ignored and suppressed (Césaire 2013, Hughes 1926, Du Bois 1903). These theories of race and ethnic studies are applied to literature to claim a position of empowerment within many different racial and ethnic cultural traditions for authors and characters within literature (Lim and Ling 1992, Krupat 1989, Anzaldúa 1987, Christian 1985). They are also used to explain the oppression, otherness, and intersecting layers of discrimination and prejudice that people of colour face in cultures characterized by a valorization of whiteness (Delgado and Stefanic 2001, Crenshaw 1995, Hull *et al.* 1982). Later writers of race theories have gone on to expose race and a range of ethnic differences as metaphors and tools used in literature to express fears about difference while simultaneously making members of minority racial or ethnic groups invisible except through these literary images. African American critic and theorist Henry Louis Gates (1985, p. 5) writes,

> Race has become a trope [or a literary figure] of ultimate, irreducible difference between cultures, linguistic groups, or practitioners of specific belief systems, who more often than not have fundamentally opposed economic interests. Race is the ultimate trope of difference because it is so very arbitrary in its application.

Applying this theory to Conrad's *Heart of Darkness*, many critics, like Chinua Achebe (1977), have noted the pervasive references to darkness and the colour black throughout the text. These images so deeply inundate readers with a fear of the unknown that by the time Marlow mentions the black bodies of Africans, they can stand for nothing but utter inhuman, irrational difference. They bear no connection to the identities or cultures of real Africans; they are metaphorical bogeymen, the embodiment of the narrator's fears. However, because the text presents them as Africans encountered on a fictional voyage made all the more real through the details gathered from Conrad's own travels, readers can integrate this damaging image of Africa into their ideas about race and Africans. These images can negate the ability of people of African descent to even claim subjectivity, a position of telling their own stories and narrating their own identities, after being so confined to the role of 'other' to white society. The underlying assumptions of race theory allow critics to expose and critique this exercise of power and discrimination in the name of narrative drama.

Many of the same issues of race and culture emerge within *postcolonial theories* as well, though these theories are compounded by the power dynamic between colonizing occupiers and the native inhabitants of colonial territories. Colonizers exercise ultimate control over colonies by imposing political, economic, educational, legal, and military institutions that destroy and replace local systems already in place. The imperial nation claims the colony as its own while constantly reminding the colonized people of their differences. Unlike the theories of African American, Latino, and Asian American schools which expose the assumptions of a society in which racial difference and inequality is maintained among citizens of shared nationalities living side-by-side, postcolonial theory explores the processes of domination from a distance as well as the modes of resistance available to people who live in two nations with two unequal cultural traditions at same time. Postcolonial theory stemming from current and former colonies throughout the world attempts to raise the visibility of these marginalized perspectives through attention to the specific modes of oppression and resistance in their contexts. Perhaps even more importantly, the theory articulates the effects of colonialism upon identity that all people in these hybrid positions share (Bhabha 1994, Appiah 1992, Spivak 1988, Said 1978, Fanon 1963).

THEORIES OF POLITICS AND CULTURE

As is evident by the summaries of the theories that focus on questions of identity, humanity, and the self, such issues overlap significantly with questions of political effects, social power, and cultural change. Whereas theories of gender and race begin with the individual identity and move out to the broader social picture, the theories of *Marxism* (Horkheimer and Adorno 2002, Macherey 1978, Eagleton 1976, Jameson 1971, Lukács 1971), *New Historicism* (Gallagher and Greenblatt 2000, Montrose 1983, Greenblatt 1980; see also Chapter 3, 'Analysis in context'), *cultural materialism* (Milner 2002, Belsey 1985, Dollimore and Sinfield 1985, Williams 1958), *ideology theory* (Žižek 1989, Althusser 1971), *cultural studies* (During 2005, Hall 1996, Foucault 1972), and *ecocriticism* (Kerridge and Sammells 1998, Glotfelty and Fromm 1996) begin with the larger social structures and seek to understand the role of literature within those networks of economic and political power. Marxist theory and the other theories it influenced see the economic system as the fundamental organizing principle of society as all humans engage in some form of labour both to ensure their survival and to produce additional capital to fuel the economy. Upon that economic base, Marxists claim, all other cultural institutions, including literature, develop, and they function either to narrate the relationship between individuals and their institutions or to offer sites of resistance where the oppressive qualities of economic systems can be exposed.

For New Historicism and the cultural studies work of Michel Foucault, the foundation of the social order is more amorphous; it is not necessarily tied to economics, but rooted in a need to establish and maintain a power structure that keeps cultures from dissolving into chaos. All of these theories see literature playing a role in both echoing the values of culture and shaping, resisting and/or reinforcing those values.

For example, a critic applying Marxist theory to Joseph Conrad's (2002) *Heart of Darkness*, originally published in *Blackwoods Magazine* in 1899, would find the representations of work and labour particularly interesting. In *Heart of Darkness*, a sailor named Marlow tells a group of gentlemen from a trading company about his past experience on the Congo River in Africa. His narrative explains how he faced a period of unemployment when he could not find work on the seas and therefore, with the help of his aunt, took a job as captain of a river steamer for a Belgian colonial trading company with interests in the Congo. His main mission was to travel upriver to retrieve one of the company's agents (Mr Kurtz) and the ivory the agent had collected. On the way, Marlow encounters European managers, directors, mechanics, and consultants, as well as African soldiers and labourers. His own crew are Africans with little knowledge of English whom the company pays in lengths of brass wire that prove worthless in securing a daily ration of food. While Marlow paints a romantic picture of his search for Kurtz as an effort to find a great man lost in a wilderness of imperial corruption and a dangerous foreign culture, the bare facts of the plot show the ways in which Marlow, Kurtz, and the African labourers are merely cogs in a global economic machine. In the end, Marlow and the company erase the disturbing details of Kurtz's violent control over the Africans who help him harvest ivory, calculate the costs of retrieving him against the profits from his ivory, and paint a picture of him as a manager with tremendous potential, but flawed strategies.

A critic applying New Historicist or ideology theories, however, might explore structures of power that extend beyond economics and wealth. The narrator's investment in the ideology of civilization, portrayed often as bringing a light into darkness, motivates many of the characters to help Marlow reach his goal. New Historicism would expose those lofty ideals as fictions designed to maintain the structure of power at the time, and a critic could then look for signs that Marlow attempts to break through that civilizing myth, but that the myth absorbs him in the end. A critic using cultural studies theories might turn from the details of Conrad's text to its adaptations into popular culture, most notably Francis Ford Coppola's *Apocalypse Now* (1979). With cultural studies assumptions about the roles of both popular and high culture texts, the critic may consider the ways in which the Vietnam War setting of *Apocalypse Now* directly parallels the mass concerns about young men seeking jobs in the colonies in Conrad's narrative. The theories do not directly make these interpretations of literary texts, but the assumptions and concepts they outline make it possible for readers to draw more connections and uncover more meanings in their own analyses.

EVERYTHING IS A CONSTRUCTION

The general outline of literary theories above groups theories based on shared questions and shared concerns. It does not clearly distinguish between the kinds of theory that were prominent in the first half of the twentieth-century and those that are more prominent today because many theories extend and develop throughout the past one hundred years. Nonetheless, a common shift in ways of thinking did take place in roughly the 1960s, and many of the earlier theories underwent a radical change in their methods and their underlying ideas. We can describe this change in intellectual paradigms as a movement from structuralism to poststructuralism.

Structuralist ways of thinking – seen, of course, in structuralist theory, but also in theories like Marxism, psychoanalysis, formalism, and even early feminist theory and race theories – seek to identify the underlying rules (or the underlying structures) that allow us to understand *all* human experience. They look for universal answers to their questions about language, identity, or society. Their theories assert large truths and attempt to tell the definitive story of how the world works. Claude Lévi-Strauss's structural anthropology offers a good example of structuralist ways of thinking. In 'The Structural Study of Myth', Lévi-Strauss (1958) first declares that all myths worldwide employ a specialized mode of language use that makes them universally translatable and grants them mythic status. Then, he uses the model of linguistics to explain that mythic language, arranging common mythic themes much like the syntax of a language or the typical parts of a narrative, such as rising action, exposition, conflict, climax, and *dénoument* or conclusion. Finally, he translates several variations of the Oedipus myth into this syntax and reduces the myths to a set of binary oppositions that he sees as fundamental to structuring the primitive human mind (e.g. life–death, family members–outsiders, earth–sky). The result is a universal rule, an answer key to understanding the myths of any human culture.

Similar grand gestures lie at the heart of other early twentieth-century theories. Early feminist theorists maintained a belief in the essential differences between men and women; they just did not think those differences made women inferior to men. Aimé Césaire's concept of *négritude* accepted the premise of an essential racial quality of blackness; he simply showed that this blackness was rich in cultural tradition, thoughtful, spiritual, sophisticated, and artistic – all those things mainstream stereotypes said people of African descent were not. Freud, as well, offered a structuralist view of human development by showing that the recognition of gender identity (and therefore human sexuality) triggered sexual repression that split our self into a conscious side and the unconscious parts we could not always control. He mapped his list of common dreams onto this developmental path and used them to assert the universal truth of the unconscious mind's obsession with sexuality and death.

For decades these rules, these statements of essential truth, seemed compelling, but the complex social developments of the mid-twentieth century (including world wars, global trade, postcolonial independence movements, and civil rights movements of all kinds) raised questions about just how 'universally' applicable they were. Freud's case studies increasingly seemed to be shaped by the rigid German and Austrian cultures of his patients. Multi-racial people and hybrid cultures demonstrated that race was not even skin deep, and women who refused the 'essential' maternal roles dictated by their biology showed the divisions between femininity and living females. Increasingly, theorists came to the conclusion that the 'universal' truths were written from a particular cultural perspective or position and that people from other perspectives would construct the same information differently and arrive at different truths. Jacques Derrida (1978) even performed a close reading of the self-contradictory language in Lévi-Strauss's essay to reveal that the units of myth were completely arbitrary and their selection based on Lévi-Strauss's own interests, and that the essay itself admitted as much.

From the 1960s to the present, all of these theories embraced the poststructuralist trend of rejecting essential truths that traditionally assume the status of 'master narratives', collective explanations we offer for history, science, knowledge, and power. Like Derrida, poststructuralists assume that no transcendent, spiritual truths that exist outside the language we use to explain our world, and many poststructuralists implicate that language within systems of domination and oppression that have often told one-sided versions of those truths. For poststructuralists, all of our truths are influenced by networks of knowledge, interpretation, and power established within societies in a particular time and place, and all can be contested by uncovering realities and truths that earlier master narratives cannot explain. Consequently, poststructuralist theories conclude that truth is a social *construction*, subject to revision and reconstruction.

In a world of reality television, Facebook, YouTube, and Twitter, the poststructuralist notion that our individual identities, subjectivities, and cultural values are constructions is, in many ways, the assumption on which our culture operates. When we read news reports that call President Barak Obama alternately too white, too black, or post-racial, we can see that there is no absolute, objective definition of race; race is a cultural construction in transition in the twenty-first century. When we witness dramatic changes in the image and identities of celebrities like Miley Cyrus, Raven-Symone, and Caitlyn Jenner, we begin to understand the ways in which we publicly perform gender roles and sexuality in order to fashion our sense of self and subjectivity as a work-in-progress. Likewise, when poststructuralist theorists talk about the 'postmodern subject' as being multiple and disconnected, we can all think of examples of presenting one image of ourselves to one group of people (e.g. employers or teachers) and a rather different persona to another group, or in another digital environment (e. g. family or friends). The lives we live everyday are poststructralist, and the most popular and vibrant theories today focus on analysing the ways in which the absence of centralizing truths makes our literature more interesting.

EVERYTHING IS A TEXT

Although this book offers a basic guide to literary analysis, in Chapter 1, 'Introduction: thinking about literature', I avoid being confined to any one definition of literature. Instead, I argue that the strategies of literary analysis can be applied to any text, any object made of words. Now I would like to return to that definition and, with the aid of theory, reconsider what it means to say we can analyse any text.

Barthes (1977, p. 156) is the first theorist to advocate using the term 'text' to explain the interdependence of writers and readers in making meaning:

> Just as Einsteinian science demands that *the relativity of the frames of reference* be included in the object studied, so the combined action of Marxism, Freudianism and structuralism demands, in literature, the relativisation of the relations of writer, reader, and observer (critic). Over against the traditional notion of the *work* ... there is now the requirement of a new object, obtained by the sliding or overturning of former categories. That object is the Text.

In poststructuralist terms, the text is the cultural construction of the object we read; its meaning emerges from the participation of readers who determine its status within society and interpret it based on the priorities of their time and place. For Barthes, conceiving literature as 'texts' opens up more possibilities than reading it as a collection of 'works', the products of authors who own and control their content. Like art in a museum, 'works' sit on bookshelves with their value and meaning intact; readers merely absorb and 'consume' this content in the same way museumgoers consume the experience of seeing the *Mona Lisa* in the Louvre from behind many layers of glass (Barthes 1977, p. 161). Pick up the same book as a 'text', however, and we flatten out the hierarchies that distinguish 'good Literature' from worthless writing (Barthes 1977, p. 157). We enter a *'social* space' in which we can play with the language, tracing its intertextual connections, following meaning down many different paths, and participating in it as readers (Barthes 1977, p. 164).

Such literary theories about texts may be full of heady abstractions, but we can see these theories in practice every day. Consider the role of various 'texts' in the 2007–2012 television series *Gossip Girl*. The series is narrated by an anonymous blogger whose posts track the lives and intrigues of wealthy teens in an elite New York City prep school. Students and informants text Gossip Girl their tips, which she reframes in stylized language (filled with intertextual references to literature and film) and texts back into the community. The characters track their social status by how much Gossip Girl talks about them and what Gossip Girl says. The public, textual (and 'texted') forum defines identities, makes or breaks reputations, and generally creates a virtual, fictional world that interacts with and influences the characters' real lives.

The final episode reveals Gossip Girl's identity in a dialogue that seems to be pulled straight from literary theory. Playing themselves, actors Rachel Bilson and Kristen Bell (the voice narrating Gossip

Girl throughout the series) read from a script for a film adaptation of the Gossip Girl blog. Their rehearsal is interrupted when Kristen Bell receives a text announcing the real identity of Gossip Girl. In response, Bilson asks, 'Wait, Gossip Girl is real?' ('New York' 2012). The characters, however, have no problem recognizing Gossip Girl's reality. In fact, they seem disappointed when the all-seeing, all-knowing virtual identity is reduced to a single, live person, character Dan Humphrey.

In his confession speech, Dan explains how he created that reality out of language – both literary and conversational – and how he used that language to create himself:

> The Upper East Side was like something from Fitzgerald or Thackeray – teenagers acting like adults, adults acting like teenagers, guarding secrets, spreading gossip, all with the trappings of truly opulent wealth. And membership in this community was so elite, you couldn't even buy your way in. It was a birthright, a birthright I didn't have and my greatest achievements would never earn me. All I had to compare to this world was what I'd read in books. But that gave me the idea. If I wasn't born into this world, maybe I could write myself into it.
>
> ('New York' 2012)

'Writing himself' into that world as 'Lonely Boy, the outsider, the underdog', Dan makes himself both the subject of the text (the writer, Gossip Girl) and its object (Lonely Boy) ('New York' 2012). He allows himself to be carried away into plots of rumours that are beyond his control. As Gossip Girl, his friends think he has been 'pulling the strings all along', and he too concludes that he 'had more power' than any of the other characters. But, of course, he didn't. Gossip Girl is a textual construction built not only from Dan's writing style and the subscribers' tips, but also from the meanings and power that readers give her. When Dan attempts to end Gossip Girl, 'she' is hacked and revived. When her identity is exposed, a writer from the next class of the prep school takes over her new outsider/insider role, writing, 'You may be rid of Dan Humphrey, but you'll never be rid of me' ('New York' 2012). More importantly, Dan and the other characters are also textual constructions as they come to embody the public roles in which Gossip Girl casts them.

With so many texts surrounding and scripting our world, our cultures, and, at times, our lives, it is not hard to see the value of literary, textual analysis. Well-known anthropologist Clifford Geertz (1979, p. 5) likens the study of culture to the work of a literary critic performing analysis on the signs and texts of everyday life:

> Believing ... that man is an animal suspended in webs of significance he himself has spun, I take culture to be those webs, and the analysis of it to be therefore not an experimental science in search of law but an interpretive one in search of meaning.

Geertz goes on to interpret the meaning of a range of rituals and cultural practices by close reading the details of the language and gestures in descriptions of cultural experiences. In turn, we can find in Geertz's conclusions about culture a purpose for our own analysis of literature.

In a poststructuralist environment, literature is a part of the social fabric, both shaped by and shaping our culture based on economics and markets, gender, sex, race, class, empire, and other structures of power. We can see literature as another of humanity's branches, a space where human experience can be explored through language, and, through analysis, we can make a place for ourselves as creators of meaning.

REFERENCES AND FURTHER READING

Achebe, C. (1977) 'An Image of Africa: Racism in Conrad's *Heart of Darkness*', *Massachusetts Review*, vol. 18, no. 4, pp. 782–794.

'The Age of Dissonance' (2009) Television program, *Gossip Girl*, CW Television Network, USA, 16 March.

Althusser, L. (1971) *Lenin and Philosophy, and Other Essays*, New York: Monthly Review Press.

Anzaldúa, G. (1987) *Borderlands/La Frontera: The New Mestiza*, San Francisco, CA: Aunt Lute Books.

Appiah, A. (1992) *In My Father's House: Africa in the Philosophy of Culture*, Oxford: Oxford University Press.

Aristotle (1997) *Poetics*, trans. M. Heath, New York: Penguin.

Barthes, R. (1972) *Mythologies*, trans. A. Lavers, New York: Hill & Wang.

Barthes, R. (1975) 'An Introduction to the Structural Analysis of Narrative', trans. L. Duisit, *New Literary History*, vol. 6, no. 2, pp. 237–272.

Barthes, R. (1977) 'From Work to Text', in S. Heath (trans. and ed.) *Image, Music, Text*, New York: Hill & Wang.

Beauvoir, S. (1953) *The Second Sex*, trans. H. M. Parshley, London: Cape.

Belsey, C. (1985) *The Subject of Tragedy: Identity and Difference in Renaissance Drama*, London: Methuen/Routledge.

Bertens, H. (2014) *Literary Theory: The Basics*, 3rd ed., London and New York: Routledge.

Bhabha, H. K. (1994) *The Location of Culture*, London and New York: Routledge.

Boileau, N. (1683) *The Art of Poetry*, trans. W. Soames and J. Dryden, London: R. Bentley and S. Magnes.

Brooks, C. (1947) *The Well Wrought Urn*, New York: Harcourt Brace.

Brooks, P. (1984) *Reading for the Plot: Design and Intention in Narrative*, New York: Knopf.

Butler, J. (1990) *Gender Trouble: Feminism and the Subversion of Identity*, New York and London: Routledge.

Césaire, A. (2013) *The Original 1939 Notebook of a Return to the Native Land: Bilingual Edition*, A. J. Arnold and C. Eshleman (trans. and ed.), Middleton, CT: Wesleyan University Press.

Christian, B. (1985) *Black Feminist Criticism: Perspectives on Black Women Writers*, New York: Pergamon Press.

Cixous, H. (1976) 'The Laugh of the Medusa', trans. K. Cohen and P. Cohen, *Signs*, vol. 1, no. 4, pp. 875–893.

Conrad, J. (2002) *Heart of Darkness and Other Tales*, ed. C. Watts, Oxford: Oxford University Press.

Corneille, P. (1862) *Oeuvres*, vol. 1, ed. C. Marty-Laveaux, Paris: Librarie de L. Hachette and Co.

Crenshaw, K. (ed.) (1995) *Critical Race Theory: The Key Writings that Formed the Movement*, New York: New Press.

Culler, J. (1992) 'Literary Theory', in J. Gibaldi (ed.) *Introduction to Scholarship in Modern Languages and Literatures*, 2nd ed., New York: The Modern Language Association of America.

Davis, L. J. (ed.) (2013) *The Disability Studies Reader*, 4th ed., New York and London: Routledge.

Delgado, R. and Stefanic, J. (2001) *Critical Race Theory: An Introduction*, New York: New York University Press.

Derrida, J. (1976) *Of Grammatology*, trans. G. C. Spivak, Baltimore, MD and London: Johns Hopkins University Press.

Derrida, J. (1978) *Writing and Difference*, trans. A. Bass, London and New York: Routledge and Kegan Paul.

Dollimore, J. and Sinfield, A (eds.) (1985) *Political Shakespeare: Essays in Cultural Materialism*, Manchester: Manchester University Press.

During, S. (2005) *Cultural Studies: A Critical Introduction*, London and New York: Routledge.

Dryden, J. (1668) *An Essay of Dramatick Poesie*, London: Henry Herringman.

Du Bois, W. E. B. (1903) *The Souls of Black Folk*, Chicago: A. C. McClurg.

Eagleton, T. (1976) *Marxism and Literary Criticism*, Berkeley: University of California Press.

Fanon, F. (1963) *The Wretched of the Earth*, trans. C. Farrington, New York: Grove Press.

Foucault, M. (1972) *The Archaeology of Knowledge and the Discourse on Language*, trans. R. Swyer, London: Tavistock.

Freud, S. (1913) *The Interpretation of Dreams*, 3rd ed., trans. A. A. Brill, New York: Macmillan.

Gallagher, C. and Greenblatt, S. (2000) *Practicing New Historicism*, Chicago: University of Chicago Press.

Gates, H. L. (1985) 'Editor's Introduction: Writing "Race" and the Difference It Makes', *Critical Inquiry*, vol. 12, no. 1, pp. 1–20.

Geertz, C. (1979) *The Interpretation of Cultures*, New York: Perseus Books.

Gilbert, S. and Gubar, S. (1979) *The Madwoman in the Attic: The Woman Writer and the Nineteenth-Century Literary Imagination*, Bloomington: Indiana University Press.

Glotfelty, C. and Fromm, H. (eds.) (1996) *The Ecocriticism Reader: Landmarks in Literary Ecology*, Athens, GA: University of Georgia Press.

Greenblatt, S. (1980) *Renaissance Self-Fashioning*, Chicago: University of Chicago Press.

Hall, S. (ed.) (1996) *Critical Dialogues in Cultural Studies*, eds. D. Morley and K. Chen, London and New York: Routledge.

hooks, b. (1984) *Feminist Theory: From Margin to Center*, Boston, MA: South End Press.

Horkheimer, M. and Adorno, T. (2002) *Dialectic of Enlightenment: Philosophical Fragments*, ed. G. S. Noerr, trans. E. Jephcott, Stanford, CT: Stanford University Press.

Hughes, L. (1926) 'The Negro Artist and the Racial Mountain', *The Nation*, vol. 23, pp. 692–694.

Hull, G. T., Scott, P. B. and Smith, B. (eds.) (1982) *But Some of Us Are Brave: Black Women's Studies*, New York: The Feminist Press.

Irigaray, L. (1985) *Speculum of the Other Woman*, trans. G. C. Gill, Ithaca, NY: Cornell University Press.

Jakobson, R. and Halle, M. (1956) *Fundamentals of Language*, The Hague: Mouton.

Jameson, F. (1971) *Marxism and Form*, Princeton, NJ: Princeton University Press.

Kerridge, R. and Sammells, N. (eds.) (1998) *Writing the Environment: Ecocriticism and Literature*, London: Zed Books.

Kristeva, J. (1980) *Desire in Language: A Semiotic Approach to Literature and Art*, ed. L. S. Roudiez, New York: Columbia University Press.

Krupat, A. (1989) *The Voice in the Margin: Native American Literature and the Canon*, Berkeley: University of California Press.

Lacan, J. (2007) *Écrits*, trans. B. Fink, New York and London: W.W. Norton.

Leavis, F. R. (1933) *For Continuity*, Cambridge: The Minority Press.

Lévi-Strauss, C. (1958) *Structural Anthropology*, London: Allen Lane.

Lim, S. G. and Ling, A. (eds.) (1992) *Reading the Literatures of Asian America*, Philadelphia: Temple University Press.

Lukács, G. (1971) *The Theory of the Novel: A Historico-Philosophical Essay on the Forms of Great Epic Literature*, trans. A. Bostock, Cambridge, MA: MIT Press.

Macherey, P. (1978) *A Theory of Literary Production*, London and New York: Routledge Kegan Paul.

Milner, A. J. (2002) *Re-Imagining Cultural Studies: The Promise of Cultural Materialism*, London: Sage.

Montrose, L. (1983) '"Shaping Fantasies": Figurations of Gender and Power in Elizabethan Culture', *Representations*, vol. 2, pp. 61–94.

Mukařowský, J. (1970) *Aesthetic Function: Norm and Value as Social Facts*, trans. M. E. Suino, Ann Arbor: University of Michigan Press.

'New York, I Love You XOXO' (2012) Television program, *Gossip Girl*, CW Television Network, USA, 17 December.

Pope, A. (1711) *An Essay on Criticism*, London, W. Lewis.

Propp, V. (1968) *Morphology of the Folktale*, trans. L. Scott, Austin: University of Texas Press.

Ransom, J. C. (1941) *The New Criticism*, New York: New Directions, 1941.

Richards, I. A. (1924) *Principles of Literary Criticism*, London: Kegan Paul, Trench, Trubner.

Said, E. (1978) *Orientalism*, New York: Pantheon.

Saussure, F. de (2011) *Course in General Linguistics*, trans. W. Baskin, New York: Columbia University Press.

Sedgwick, E. K. (1985) *Between Men: English Literature and Male Homosocial Desire*, New York: Columbia University Press.

Shelley, P. B. (1840) *Essays, Letters from Abroad, Translations, and Fragments*, London: Edward Moxon.

Shklovsky, V. (1991) *Theory of Prose*, trans. B. Sher, Normal, IL: Dalkey Archive Press.

Showalter, E. (1977) *A Literature of Their Own: British Women Novelists from Brontë to Lessing*, Princeton, NJ: Princeton University Press.

Spivak, G. C. (1988) 'Can the Subaltern Speak', in C. Nelson and L. Grossberg (eds.) *Marxism and the Interpretation of Culture*, London: Macmillan.

Waugh, P. (ed.) (2006), *Literary Theory and Criticism: An Oxford Guide*, New York: Oxford University Press.

Williams, R. (1958) *Culture and Society 1780–1950*, London: Chatto & Windus.

Woolf, V. (1981) *A Room of One's Own*, New York: Harcourt Brace Jovanovich.

Wordsworth, W. (1800) *Lyrical Ballads with Other Poems*, vol. 1, London: N. Longman and O. Rees.

Žižek, S. (1989) *The Sublime Object of Ideology*, London: Verso.

7

CONCLUSION: ANALYTICAL WRITING

In May 2014, *The New York Times* printed 13 lines of poetry on the front page. It was not a slow news day. The lines from 'On the Pulse of Morning', the 1993 poem for the inauguration of Bill Clinton, were part of a tribute to Maya Angelou whose obituary was one of the longest to make the front-page in recent *Times* history. The online version of the article featured links to an array of tribute editorials, embedded comments from readers, a slideshow of 10 images, and three video clips: one of Angelou reading 'Phenomenal Woman' (1978) over a photomontage spanning many decades; the next an interview with Khalil Muhammad, Director of the Schomberg Center for Research in Black Culture, discussing Angelou's manuscripts; and finally a clip from the presidential inauguration, featuring her poem. Her celebrity-studded funeral, arguably the most-watched in literary history, demonstrated the vast social impact of this beloved writer of *I Know Why the Caged Bird Sings* (1969) and other memoirs, poetry, and essays.

A similar, multi-article memorial tribute to novelist Beryl Bainbridge appeared in *The Guardian* in 2010. Clearly, discussing literature is not just for term papers.

The strategies of literary analysis outlined throughout this book may be applied anywhere – in conversations or just for yourself in the privacy of your own home – but the best literary analyses contribute to a public dialogue carried on in writing. As described in

Chapter 5, 'Analysis and the critics', examples of literary **criticism** fill our environment. Media and formats vary widely from formal newspaper and magazine reviews to video and audio broadcasts and creative, hypertext, multimedia digital forms. Even informal venues like blogs, the #bookreview Twitter hashtag, comment posts on news articles, online rankings in bookshops like Amazon, and customer reviews of books or films all provide spaces for public analysis of literary texts.

When a writer creates a well-crafted argument that expands upon the meanings of an original text, that analysis can enhance the excitement and discovery of the initial reading experience. This chapter offers an overview of the process of synthesis that brings together various strategies of analysis into coherent arguments about literature both for academic audiences and for the wider world.

ACADEMIC WRITING ABOUT LITERATURE

Like all of the other texts we read, academic writing follows specific **generic convention**s. Academic arguments about literature should include a thoughtful purpose related to expanding knowledge about the **text** or texts, a clear argument about how the text works and why it works that way, a focused and powerful thesis that states the point of the argument, thorough body paragraphs that support the thesis with analytical **close reading**s of detailed examples, and a conclusion that reveals what we have gained by exploring in-depth interpretations throughout the essay.

PURPOSE

At their most basic level, all academic arguments about literature aim to convince others to share an interpretation of the text. In academic settings, these arguments may be completely open to students' own interpretations, or they may be limited by particular assignments: explications, comparisons, critical responses, contextual or cultural analyses, or applications of theoretical concepts. Whatever the prompt for academic writing, the purpose must expand beyond the assigned task. Academic writers must determine how they are contributing to our shared knowledge about the meanings of texts, and must let that purpose guide the tone and direction of the argument.

For example, an academic writer may be required to produce an explication (which is like an exegesis), a line-by-line, detailed analysis of the implied meanings within a poem or short passage from a longer text. All explications follow the lines in order, calling attention to formal structures, figurative language, word choices, and implied meanings, but each explication's purpose will depend upon the interpretations revealed through analysis. Will the explication of the details of a passage expose an underlying theme (e.g. blindness in *Oedipus the King*), reveal an ironic undercurrent in a seemingly straightforward passage (e.g. concern that Ophelia and Hamlet are growing too romantically entwined in *Hamlet*), or point out a recurring image that hints at a larger concern within the text (e.g. the role of careless drivers in *The Great Gatsby*)? Other academic tasks, like comparisons or cultural analyses, may have their purpose built in, but academic writers must still refine it. Will a comparison of seemingly different texts reveal an enduring position on a common theme? Will a contextual analysis demonstrate that the text defies cultural norms or supports them? Connecting the argument to a specific intellectual purpose can mean the difference between uninspired and insightful academic writing.

ARGUMENT AND THESIS

Developing analytical arguments about literature demands that writers balance close readings of textual details with bigger picture meanings. The most powerful academic arguments begin with the passages that prove most interesting or relevant to the question posed by a particular prompt. Then, only after close reading the passages do academic writers identify the patterns that link them and refine these patterns into an overarching claim about their meaning. Thus, although a written academic argument explains the thesis in the introduction and provides the close readings in body paragraphs, the process of developing the analysis takes place in reverse.

The 1816 Romantic poem 'On First Looking into Chapman's Homer' by John Keats (2007, p. 12), describes the difference between hearing about Homer's poetry written in Greek and reading Chapman's English translation of Homer for himself. Written in sonnet form, the poem first describes the speaker as a traveller circling 'round many western islands' but never landing in the wide kingdom 'Homer ruled' until he read Chapman (Keats 2007, p. 12). The second half of the poem changes tone utterly. Inspired by Chapman's 'loud and bold' speech, the speaker becomes an astronomer, a sailor and explorer, a discoverer of radically new spaces far beyond those western islands that are part of the god Apollo's poetic kingdom (Keats 2007, p. 12). Analysing these details can lead to several possible arguments.

To craft a thesis statement, we link the patterns of meaning found in the details to a significant concern or debate within the critical conversation. We can identify those debates either by researching and responding to the critics or more simply by relating our interpretations to common questions within the field of literary studies about the cultural, historical, literary, linguistic, psychological, and philosophical effects of literature. Building upon our analysis of Keats's poem, we can tie that analysis to broad literary questions in order to make a claim about the value of the meanings we see. For each of the following questions, I include an example of a thesis statement that enters the critical conversation on the basis of our close reading above.

- *How does the text's meaning relate to its genre? Does it follow or break generic conventions?* By exploiting the traditional break in the sonnet structure, 'On First Looking into Chapman's Homer' highlights the evolution and awakening of the speaker's consciousness and poetic development as he reads Homer in English for the first time.
- *How does the text's meaning relate to the conventions and concerns of its literary period?* Although John Keats describes an epiphany achieved through reading, 'On First Looking into Chapman's Homer' depicts a physical journey that parallels the Romanticists' many spiritual awakenings achieved through a connection with nature.
- *How does the text's meaning relate to its literary movement?* The Romantics valued personal reflection and asserted that poems emerge from individual emotional experiences. John Keats's 'On First Looking into Chapman's Homer' exemplifies the Romantic emphasis on the superiority of the direct experience by valorizing the act of reading in English over second-hand knowledge of the Greek classics.
- *How does awareness of the text's cultural and social* **context** *transform its meaning?* In John Keats's 'On First Looking into Chapman's Homer', Chapman's translation of Homer effectively negates social class differences for Keats by making the classics available to the middle classes who are not educated to read Greek. This poem celebrates the speaker's 'discovery' of direct access to artistic culture.

TEXTUAL EVIDENCE

Once the overall argument is encapsulated in a thesis statement, the academic writer reassembles and reorganizes the textual details and close readings that led to the argument in the first place. The body paragraphs may include close readings of the narrative structure, the interactions among characters, the use of literary figures and images – all of the details discussed in Chapter 2, 'Close reading: words and forms'.

In our sample argument about the text's use of the sonnet genre, for example, the thesis offers clear directions about the kind of evidence we must provide in the body paragraphs. We must demonstrate first that the poem follows a conventional Petrarchan sonnet structure with a rhymed octet that introduces an idea and a differently-rhymed sestet that responds to the initial premise. In this case, we want to emphasize the radical shift in word choice, sentence structure, and tone from the octet to the sestet. By calling attention to the surprising choice of the word 'bold' immediately before the stanza break, we can support our argument that the poem describes an evolution or change (Keats 2007, p. 12). We can then focus on the images of discovery in the second half to characterize that change as an awakening.

In academic arguments about literature, New Critical principles continue to guide the content of body paragraphs. New Critics called it a *fallacy*, a mistake in logic, to write about the author's intentions or the reader's emotional response, and today's academic readers continue to disparage references to authors' thoughts or readers' feelings. Comments about what the author wanted or meant to say are labelled *intentional fallacies* because we cannot know what the author intended simply by reading the text, and, for New Critics, even evidence of the author's intentions stated directly in journals or interviews cannot fully explain what the text accomplishes (see Chapter 1, 'Introduction: thinking about literature'). A second New Critical term, the *affective fallacy*, refers to the readers' 'affect' or emotions and the logical error of using those emotions to support an analytical argument. Academic audiences reject comments about how readers may feel about or relate to texts because they are examples of affective fallacies. Such comments reveal only how one person feels; they do not prove what a text means.

Furthermore, while literary analysis arguments may discuss moral choices and social issues or even indirectly teach lessons about ourselves, the purpose must remain analysis. Literary analysis centres upon the way language attempts to represent human experiences and how readers can find meaning within those **representation**s, and the evidence presented in the body paragraphs must reveal how the text works and why it works that way, not why some characters' actions are deplorable or pitiful.

Throughout this book, I have modelled the use of quotes and other textual evidence from literary and critical sources to support my interpretations. I have also followed the conventions of the Harvard Referencing Style to give credit to those sources and to indicate which references are quotes, paraphrases, and summaries. Different academic contexts may require different rules for citing sources (e.g. Chicago Style, MLA Style, APA Style), but this usually means little more than a rearrangement of punctuation and dates. Combining detailed close readings with a careful attention to citing textual evidence will establish academic credibility and offer powerful support for the analytical argument.

CONCLUSIONS

Public speakers often conclude with repetition and review, sometimes even reiterating earlier points verbatim to help their listeners recall what they have heard. Such repetition is generally unnecessary in written arguments where readers can refer back to earlier parts of the text. Instead, conclusions of academic arguments should reinforce the underlying purpose of the argument and point out what readers have gained by examining the details within the body paragraphs.

For example, our argument begins with the thesis about the sonnet genre: By exploiting the traditional break in the sonnet structure, 'On First Looking into Chapman's Homer' highlights the evolution and awakening of the speaker's consciousness and poetic development as he reads Homer in English for the first time. The body paragraphs carefully explore the particular types of awakening the poem describes: an evolution from the constraints of feudal poetic dominions to the far more democratic freedom of new worlds opened by scientific and geographical discovery. After leading the argument down those politically-charged paths of interpretation, the academic writer cannot conclude simply that there is an awakening. The political significance of the metaphors of awakening connect

Keats's sonnet to a larger project of human freedom. By comparing poetic creativity to scientific progress in the poem's second half, the poem uses the break between the sonnet's octet and sestet to announce a break from old poetry and an embrace of the new. The significance of the analysis and the conclusion we may draw, is that a poem about being indebted to past poets actually leaps over them and breaks new poetic boundaries.

THE POPULAR CRITIC: WRITING ABOUT LITERATURE IN THE WORLD

Comic Eddie Izzard's performance, *Definite Article* (1996), opens with Izzard emerging from the centre of a giant, stage-wide book, giving literature a spotlight as the only prop throughout the entire show. Leading into an analysis of Robert Burns's line, 'The best laid schemes o' Mice an' Men/Gang aft agley', Izzard notes that 'Poetry is very similar to music, only less notes and more words' (*Definite Article* 1996). He then mocks readers' tendencies to view poetic lines as deep and profound by attempting to envision a real mouse's well-laid plan. The joke depends on his audience's ability to appreciate the poem seriously and to recognize the ways Izzard plays with and disrupts the rules of literary analysis in this popular, comedic context.

Interviewing poet Elizabeth Alexander in 2009, comedian Stephen Colbert of *The Colbert Report* opened with an ironic, but profound literary question, 'Poems aren't true, are they? They're made up, right?' In a surprising move for a comedy show, Colbert spends the next six minutes on a tongue-in-cheek, but generally accurate, discussion of poetry aimed at introducing viewers to Alexander's poem, 'Praise Song for the Day', delivered at President Barack Obama's inauguration the previous day. In the course of their discussion, Alexander clarifies that 'a poem should be true in some way: emotionally true, true to the language that it has' (*Colbert* 2009). The show also gives her time to define metaphor as 'a way of using language where you make a comparison to let people understand something as it relates to something else, and that's how you use language to increase meaning' (*The Colbert Report* 2009). Although Colbert jokingly refers to them as 'metaphor-lies', throughout the interview he quotes poetry from T. S. Eliot and William Shakespeare; effectively defines the term 'praise song'; and offers the example of 'We Don't Need Another Hero', the theme song to the film *Mad Max: Beyond Thunderdome* (1985), to explain that an 'occasional poem' is a poem written in honour of a particular event or occasion (*The Colbert Report* 2009). The examples may be outlandish, but when Colbert invites Alexander to 'talk about meaning for a second', they genuinely do (*The Colbert Report* 2009). The satirical talk show produces real, popular culture literary analysis.

Like the Izzard and Colbert examples, many non-academic kinds of writing about literature, including reviews, apply the strategies of analysis in popular contexts. Their language may be less formal. Their citations may be more fluid. But ultimately these popular culture forms follow many of the same generic conventions as academic literary analysis.

PURPOSE

While academic writing must serve an intellectual purpose, popular literary analysis can be more diverse; it can praise or condemn, recommend, or link texts to current cultural events. Neither intentional fallacies nor affective fallacies apply in popular analysis, and learning more about authors or describing emotional responses may be the whole purpose of analysis. The many responses to Maya Angelou's death demonstrate this range of purposes. The central obituary in *The New York Times*, 'Maya Angelou, Lyrical Witness to the Jim Crow South, Dies', seeks to honour her accomplishments both as a writer and as a leader in the civil rights movement (Fox 2014, p. A1). Elizabeth Alexander's more academic tribute published the same day focuses on Angelou's role in forging a path for African American women writers by proving her story could attract millions of readers. In contrast, Charles M. Blow, a regular commentator on politics and social justice, takes a personal approach, expressing his deep gratitude for the role model Angelou provided him.

ARGUMENT AND THESIS

With greater freedom of purpose, popular writers of literary analysis need not base their thesis statements solely upon close readings. The thesis statements of our three examples reveal the connections between the writers' purpose and their statements of the overall argument. The journalistic obituary connects literature and culture in a thesis with an informative and evaluative tone:

> Throughout her writing, Ms Angelou explored the concepts of personal identity and resilience through the multifaceted lens of race, sex, family, community and the collective past. As a whole, her work offered a clear-eyed examination of the ways in which the socially marginalizing forces of racism and sexism played out at the level of the individual.
>
> (Fox 2014, A1)

In contrast, Alexander's thesis conveys the value she places upon the African American literary tradition and especially the role of women's voices within it:

> [S]he rendered not only her own life visible but also nothing short of a history of black social movements in the second half of the 20th century and the participation of a woman, and women, who helped make it happen, against a million odds …. The success of Ms Angelou's memoir helped clear a path for the boom in black women's writing, and the success of writers like Toni Morrison, Alice Walker, Ntozake Shange, Gloria Naylor and Toni Cade Bambara, among many others.

Alexander's thesis says less about Angelou as a person than it does about the effects *I Know Why the Caged Bird Sings* and other texts produced in the lives of readers. As one of those readers, Blow grew up, like Angelou, with his own African American grandmother in the same rural Arkansas Angelou writes about in her most famous book. Blow's (2014) thesis highlights the impact of her memoir in intimate terms: 'Reading her words, for the first time, I could see myself and my life in literature'. In many ways, his thesis echoes Alexander's – Angelou gave voice to an experience previous literature had ignored – but Blow measures those effects in individual lives, not in the **literary canon**.

For these writers of popular literary analysis, the power of the thesis stems from its ability to tap into larger cultural concerns and experiences and to offer arguments with which their readers can identify.

TEXTUAL EVIDENCE

The same kind of textual evidence used in academic literary analysis appears in popular analysis as well. Throughout the obituary,

Fox (2014, p. A1) cites lines from Angelou's poetry and memoirs, quotes comments from critics, and in the online version of the story, even offers links to poetry readings. Colbert, Blow, and Alexander all use similar evidence. Short, well-chosen quotes surrounded by commentary make the analysis accessible to readers and support its argument without revealing so much of the texts that the readers feel the enjoyment of reading it would be spoiled.

In a discussion of literature on the *PoemTalk* podcast, literary critic Dee Morris offers an excellent model of selective quoting and commentary for popular audiences. *PoemTalk* podcasts combine audio clips of short poetry readings, followed by a conversation about the poem among invited poets, scholars, professors, and critics, but the audience is not academic. The conversations are detailed, the guests highly knowledgeable, but their dialogue is accessible to anyone interested in poetry; at times, it is humorous and fun. Commenting on lines from H.D.'s *Helen in Egypt* (1961), Morris notes that the poem builds its 'narrative on the model of an onion' (Filreis 2015). The metaphor fittingly describes H.D.'s poem which tracks the famed Helen of Troy's life through an alternate plot in which the gods hid her in Egypt and left a phantom copy to carry on at the war in Troy. The poem then peels back the onion-like layers of intrigue surrounding Helen – the false Helen's infidelity, the Greek soldiers' resentment of her, the gods' manipulation of her image, and her own real story, set in Egypt. Again, Morris uses clear and common language to offer a close reading that reveals the overall meaning of the poem. Morris notes that Helen 'calls Thetis "sea-mother", but if you destabilize that word by just listening to the sound of it, it's "seem other," and this whole 300-page poem has to do with things that we thought we know, seen in some other way in which they "seem other"' (Filreis 2015). To this comment, the host replies with a somewhat awestruck, 'Wow' (Filreis 2015).

Throughout this podcast, Morris's quotes are quite short, but her selections hint at the character and style of the whole poem. Her insightful explanations draw upon deconstruction, feminist theory, poetics, and a range of specialist knowledge, but her words do not: the poem holds onto meaning like an onion; the repeated sound of sea-mother tells us why we need to peel the onion in the first place.

CONCLUSIONS

In popular writing, the conclusions mirror the purpose and thesis, though often with more of a dramatic flourish than their academic counterparts. Drawing upon journalistic conventions, Fox (2014, p. A1) ends her article with a hint of conflict, noting the sometimes lacklustre reviews Angelou received about her work, but Fox's final anecdote about the beginning of *I Know Why the Caged Bird Sings* confirms Angelou's indomitable spirit and tremendous accomplishments. As opinion writers, Alexander and Blow share the same soaring rhetoric, though in the end Blow uses emotional language and Alexander invokes the inspiration of Angelou's poetry. In all cases, the conclusions either state or imply the significance of the larger argument, just as they do in academic writing.

In all their variations, literary analyses have the capacity to make the effects of literature more knowable, more understandable, and ultimately greater. By amplifying the meanings, slowing down the reading process, savouring the details of the text, literary analysis performs a valuable service for readers, and it ensures that fresh interpretations will always continue to keep our literature alive.

REFERENCES AND FURTHER READING

Alexander, E. (2014) 'In a Commanding Voice, Singing Out to the World', *The New York Times*, 28th May, p. A27.

Angelou, M. (1969) *I Know Why the Caged Bird Sings*, New York: Random House.

Blow, C. M. (2014) 'Maya and Me and Maya: What Maya Angelou Meant to Me', *The New York Times*, [Online] 28th May. Available from: http://nytimes.com. [Accessed 30th May 2015].

The Colbert Report. (2009), Television program, Comedy Central, 21st January.

Definite Article. (1996) Film. Directed by Ed Bye. [VHS] UK: Vision Video.

Filreis, A. (2015) 'The I as Hieroglyph: H.D. *Helen in Egypt*', Podcast, *Poem Talk*, Philadelphia, Pennsylvania, 27th January, Available from: http://jacket2.org/podcasts/i-hieroglyph-poemtalk-84. [Accessed 13th November 2015].

Fox, M. (2014) 'Maya Angelou, Lyrical Witness of the Jim Crow South, Dies', *The New York Times*, 28th May, p. A1.

H.D. (1961) *Helen in Egypt*, New York: Grove Press.

Keats, J. (2007) *Selected Poems*, ed. J. Barnard, New York: Penguin.

GLOSSARY

affective fallacy   a principle of New Criticism that discounts consideration of a text's emotional effects on readers

allusion   an indirect reference to another **text**, often one of **canonical** stature or from popular culture. Seen in uncredited incorporation of lines, images, or characters from other sources.

author   the person responsible for originating a **text**, including the writer or writers of written texts, the creators of the written portions of multimedia texts (such as screenplays, song and opera lyrics, or comic script), and the storytellers of **oral literature**. Used in Romanticism to refer to the creative genius of literary work, but viewed as a conduit for culture, language, and information by twentieth-century literary theorists.

canon   a set of texts considered to provide a definitive representation of the range of literary accomplishment throughout history. Used to signal the value and importance of a small group of texts over other, less central ones.

canonical   belonging to the highly valued texts within the **canon**.

classic   a text with enduring influence, relevance, and readership. Used to refer to texts considered to be masterpieces of literary technique whose language and content retain their power and value over generations or centuries.

close reading   a method of careful analysis developed by New Critics to focus upon the underlying meanings of the words in a **text**. Includes quoting individual lines of text and commenting on those lines to interpret multiple meanings and histories of words, formal and stylistic elements, and figurative language.

context   the character and experience of the time, place, and culture in which a **text** is written and published. Includes the literary context of the other texts that are popular at the time, the political and legal climate, technological developments, cultural values, level of **literacy**, and social institutions governing human activity.

convention   the set of typical features traditionally associated with a particular literary **genre**, subgenre, or form.

critic   a person, often a scholar, fellow author, or editor, who evaluates and interprets texts, especially in print.

criticism   the act of analysing, interpreting, and evaluating the underlying meaning of texts. Also used to refer to the written essays, articles, and books that express such interpretations.

figurative language   words used for purposes other than communicating basic definitions. Includes puns, metaphors, and other figures of speech that distort or add to the literal meanings of words by focusing attention upon the form of the word rather than taking for granted its transparent definition.

figures of speech   (see **figurative language**)

generic convention   (see **convention**)

genre   category or type of literature, such as poetry, drama, prose. Recognized by common **conventions** of length, style, form, content, and other features.

intentional fallacy   a principle of New Criticism that discounts the **author**s' desired message in favour of the meanings readers can interpret from the finished text. Used to refer to the error of viewing the meaning of the text as a coded message from the author.

intertextuality   the web of interrelationships among **texts** of various times and contexts, including indebtedness to earlier plots, common metaphors, idioms, and other literary figures, and other influences and repetitions of language.

literacy   the ability to read and write.

literary associated with language used with attention to form, not only for direct communication. Used as a synonym for *belles lettres*, beautiful words.

literary canon (see **canon**)

literary figure (see **figurative language**)

literary movement a set of **author**s and **text**s produced by a community of writers with shared goals for changing the purpose, form, and/or definition of literature.

literary period a historical division of literature into centuries or generations which share similar cultural trends, popular literary **genre**s, related literary movements, common **literacy** rates and publishing practices, broad intellectual and philosophical perspectives, and responses to world events.

literary theorist (see **theorist**)

literary theory (see **theory**)

lyric, lyrical associated with personal, often emotional, reflection expressed in highly **figurative language**. Used in classical poetry to refer to poetry accompanied by the music of a lyre, sung by a single poet from his or her first-person perspective.

movement (see **literary movement**)

narrative a series of events or experiences organized and described by a speaker (in poetry) or narrator (in prose or other genres). Used in classical literary theory to distinguish a **text** that offered an external account of events from **lyric**s that offered a personal reflection or **drama** that did not describe events, but performed them directly with actors.

oral literature a **genre** of literature designed to be distributed by word of mouth, not in written publications. Used to refer to literature produced prior to the development of written language or as a supplement or counter-tradition to written literature and shared within a community by storytellers or through song.

performance an oral, visual, and/or physical presentation of a **text**. Used to emphasize the role of the movements, voices, and appearance of the actors or storytellers that act in concert with the words of a text, especially in the genres of drama and oral literature.

period (see **literary period**)

prose a **genre** of literature characterized by continuous sentences arranged in paragraphs, as distinguished from lines of poetry arranged in **verse**.

representation   in literature, the process of calling forth the reality of an experience or object through the medium of language, thus all literature is *about* reality rather than *being* reality. Also used to refer to the object or image created in language that replaces and stands for the objects in the real world.

text   an object composed of language that can be read or heard, often a publication, but also performed texts (such as plays or films), or visual texts (such as ads or works of art). Used to refer to objects to which interpretive strategies of literary analysis can be applied.

theorist   a writer of texts used to answer fundamental questions about the nature of literature and language. Used to distinguish from a **critic** who produces interpretations of particular **text**s.

theory   a set of texts and concepts from a variety of fields of study that explain and define underlying assumptions about literature, reading, language, and meaning as a whole. Used to distinguish from **criticism** which analyses and interprets particular texts.

verse   a formal and purposeful arrangement of words in which the length of the line, rhythm, and other sound patterns are deliberately organized, not determined by the size and shape of the paper on which they are printed. Used to differentiate from **prose** and often as a synonym for poetry. Also can refer to a single line of poetry within a stanza.

INDEX

CPSIA information can be obtained
at www.ICGtesting.com
Printed in the USA
LVHW081103180119
604215LV00013BA/107/P